1-7

AKe→10-41

Manuel→232-246

Blues for New Orleans

THE CITY IN THE TWENTY-FIRST CENTURY
Eugenie L. Birch and Susan M. Wachter, Series Editors

A complete list of books in the series is available from the publisher.

Blues for New Orleans

Mardi Gras and America's Creole Soul

ROGER D. ABRAHAMS, WITH
NICK SPITZER,
JOHN F. SZWED, AND
ROBERT FARRIS THOMPSON

PENN

University of Pennsylvania Press

Philadelphia

10   9   8   7   6   5   4   3   2   1

Published by
University of Pennsylvania Press
Philadelphia, Pennsylvania 19104-4112

A Cataloging-in-Publication Record is available from the Library of Congress

Contents

Introduction

When you get to New Orleans, then you'll know what Carnival's for!

There is no more powerful symbol of life in New Orleans and the region around it than Mardi Gras. The annual festival along the central Gulf Coast of Louisiana, Mississippi, and Alabama is an emblem of the area's historical and cultural difference from the rest of the South. It also connects America's "Third Coast" to the Old Worlds of Mediterranean Europe, West Africa, and Native America. Mardi Gras ("Fat Tuesday"), or Carnival ("farewell to fleshly excess"), includes such events as costumed float parades, neighborhood marches or second-lines, street gatherings, informal parties, and formal balls in New Orleans, Biloxi, and Mobile, among other Gulf Coast cities and towns. In rural French southwest Louisiana, a Cajun and black Creole *courir de Mardi Gras* or Mardi Gras run is carried out by horseback-mounted revelers in more than a dozen communities.

The city of New Orleans was once the nexus and cultural jewel of the French, and Spanish Caribbean, the North America colonies, and later the American South. The cultural and linguistic elements that interpenetrated and mixed in the city turned it into a center of creative cultural sources the likes of which the United States has never seen again—what folklorist Alan Lomax called the Athens of the New World. The best way to begin thinking about New Orleans as the rarified crossroads of artistic development in this hemisphere is to adjust our sense of geography, and visualize the city not as the bottom of the United States, but as the crown of the Caribbean. From this perspective, the entire city, its cultures, its musics, and its Mardi Gras, comes into intercontinental focus and takes on a new aura.

Although jazz from the city traveled north, east, and west just after the turn of the century, first in the hands of French Creole piano professor Jelly Roll Morton and later in the singular trumpet solos of African American Louis Armstrong and the bluesy vibrato of Creole clarinetist Sidney Bechet, it is in Carnival that music must ultimately be celebrated as a totality in the city's nineteenth-century spider web grid of streets. This is the time when all classes and cultures animate the space both by asserting their turf and going where they shouldn't, sometimes to show what they are not supposed to in this special time and place. Carnival is New Orleans' most commanding symbol of culture as both organized and chaotic, individual and collective, accepted and licentious, sacredly situated on the calendar and profanely profound. Carnival—especially the black carnival of the Mardi Gras Indians, the Zulu Parades, the Baby Dolls and Bonesmen—has its home base in many of the neighborhoods that have been drowned by the recent natural disasters and political failings.

In the wake of the flood and its sad aftermath, the Associated Press asked a poignant question, "As black New Orleanians regroup and put down roots elsewhere—some temporary, some not—many wonder: What will become of one of the nation's most complex African-American cultures." The answer, alas, may come from bureaucrats who have never understood the complexity of the question—those who think in blunt racial terms of black and white without regard for culture, those who are hamstrung and mudslung by the disaster that every hydrologist, climatologist, and geologist in the region has predicted for three decades. In Louisiana there will be the traditional American upstate-downstate face-off, based here in the distinctions of the Anglo/Afro-Southern north and Afro-French Mediterranean south. Nationally, there is and will be sufficient finger pointing within the various private and government agencies that will bumble around wondering who's eligible for the moneys raised or allocated. If none of the neighborhoods built on the lowest grounds are left standing, or more significantly if few of their residents return, no carnival will occur as we know it. No carnival, no New Orleans, and America's syncopated soul counterpoint to the increasingly acultural and monocultural mainstream will disappear.

We recognize the complexity here. There are African Americans from inundated Gentilly to the Ninth Ward and New Orleans East who assert that no festivities can go forward when the dead are barely recovered, the housing about to be condemned, three-fourths of the city a dark and quiet carcass. There is a claim that, with only the famous French Quarter, Garden District, and Uptown high and dry, it is unseemly to celebrate against a backdrop of suffering. Others—black, white, and Creole—counter that Mardi Gras means work for busboys and waiters, float-makers and King Cake bakers—that it is the symbol of joy and life in the city. Pragmatists add that, even if Mardi Gras has these economic benefits and provides needed balm to the soul and spirit of natives and visitors alike, America just doesn't understand the celebration or the city and will lose its shot at federal funds, Category 5 levees, and restored wetlands. Our sense is that there will be Mardi Gras—and that even if limited in scale by scarcity of the citizenry or issues of decorum, it will artistically encapsulate this bizarre cultural moment in a manner that embraces both the concerns for appropriateness and need for the pleasure of the music and parades, feasting, and fleshy excess it embodies for the public that can assemble. In this sense, we cast no arrows at those who choose to not participate and even object, nor at those who join the parade of saints and sinners in defiance of the odds. Still, this does not mean we are not in arms with all New Orleans kith and kin in our fury at the confederacy of failures that has brought us to this conflicted moment.

The old adage "It's easier to be angry together than by yourself" has much going for it, especially when it comes to considering the government's response to a flood caused by engineering malfeasance, its aftermath, and the perilous future of New Orleans. At least for the authors of this book, our anger was kindled forty years ago or more by the insistent neglect of African and other non-Western European cultural traditions that have been nurtured and maintained in the New World. The emotion and hope for inclusion of the great expressive culture our diversity has produced have kindled a good deal of talk and writing on our parts. The idea of a plural culture with an inclusiveness of people and their expressions that developed from the Civil Rights movement has entered a new phase, particularly in the mercantile centers engendered by the global marketplace. Now, in the face of recent events, the exercise of cultural difference seems more like an argument for human rights. Cultures, especially in their most vernacular renderings, clearly have ignored political boundaries, as the history of creole communities in and beyond Louisiana shows.

The New Orleans that has so affected American life is not just the open city of Mardi Gras, it is also the city of the working poor, with the dreams Tennessee Williams gave us in *Streetcar Named Desire*. It is a port of entry for the Old World that once rivaled New York in size. Mark Twain called it one of the great American cities (along with New York, Boston, and San Francisco). Beyond the colonial French and Spanish period, and the downriver drift of the "Kaintucks" and other Américains, New Orleans became the catch basin for escaping Old World populations of the nineteenth and twentieth centuries, the Germans, Irish, and Sicilians (the latter depicted by E. Annie Proulx in *Accordion Crimes*). The regional writer Harnett Kane would call this New Orleans the unifying gumbo pot of mingled civilizations, "A poetic city with a prosaic population." The gentler Eudora Welty saw New Orleans as "the place where the firm ground ceases and the unsound footing begins. . . . A certain kind of person likes such a place. A certain kind of person wants to go there and never leave." (Not that the more inward Miss Welty was one of them.) And it has been the location of wonder for southern whites like William Faulkner, who declared of the visual splendors of the place, "I love three things: gold; marble and purple; splendor, solidity, color," when beginning his vignettes on New Orleans of the 1920s. Faulkner here is paying appropriate tribute to the colors of the official Mardi Gras flag, green, gold, and purple standing for faith, power, and justice.

We will mention many others of these wonders as we go along, though not with footnotes. Forgive us: as academics driven by the urgency of recent events to produce this book in record time, we felt that we wanted the liberating force of the moment. We wanted for once to share in the liberties taken by Mardigridians—the word for the black Mardi Gras Indians given by Donald Harrison, the late and great Big Chief of the Guardians of the Sacred Flame masking group—the word we dare to extend to all the carnival's celebrants.

While pulling our ideas together, we are reminded of how many, like Harrison, have shared their understandings and their enthusiasms, some of them fellow-scholars, old Mardigridians. Many energetic researchers have been active in searching out the contours of transatlantic cultural continuities and inventions. Our colleagues and students have repeatedly discovered seats of vernacular vigor where plantations and their trade once flourished, places in which the confrontations of class and race have been translated, at least in the form of holiday festivities, into cultural performances and artifacts that have become part of the world's legacy of stylistic endeavor. Now, with Mardi Gras and the carnival spirit shifted and shifting into diaspora neighborhoods in other cities throughout the world, the prospect of what will become of these traditions and the city they create seems hazy and mysterious.

Working together by long distance, we are also reminded of how much has been left out of the complex, nuanced, and ultimately creolized record of black/white relations because of a failure to think across national borders and include persistently localized communities of historically African-related peoples. A review of the writings on African American communities and the close-up observations of ethnographers reveal a great many similarities between far-flung diasporic colonies, similarities that go well beyond and even exceed anything we could have predicted during the Civil Rights era. The historical record of Mardi Gras in many ways resonates with the experience of festivities throughout what was once the "plantation world." These revelries were created out of traditions of resistance as much as they were from activities that enhance life's continuities. These were not simple reflexive responses to enslavement. To the contrary, they were well-organized moments, complex mnemonic and expansive efforts to maintain face, body, spirit among those still living after the harshness of slavery. As with festive celebrations or rituals everywhere, they provided a time in which history could be replayed, ancestral styles and subjects reinforced, and new power roles developed that proved incredibly long-lived after emancipation. From these holidays emerged organized mass escapes into the bush and swamps, especially where Maroon (runaway) communities had already been established. Little wonder that the plantation authorities repeatedly attempted to legislate against these celebrations.

Today, festivities are held throughout the ex-plantation world that mark such historical moments and often conceal a continuing connection to Africa. Mardi Gras is one of many occasions that celebrate these events away from the tourists and the Uptown revelers, in the festivities that are carried out in the mostly Afro-Creole, African American Seventh, Eighth, and Ninth Wards of New Orleans.

Ours is an outrage of the moment over the devastation initiated by natural disaster and compounded by the failure of the government at every level to prepare for an occurrence that had been foretold since the building of this city in an unstable coastal environment, We are angry in the face of a hurricane whose intensity blew away many of our dreamscapes, and even angrier because human intervention could have prevented it in a way most natural disasters cannot be. And now, we daily witness the indignities issuing from those who run our national lives, as they ask, "What's left to reconstruct? Let's just start all over." Without raising taxes. This is pure ignorance of a natural and cultural disaster of the grandest proportion in our country's history.

In the aftermath of the storm's winds, surge, and flood, we are faced with losing our greatest vernacular creation, the City of New Orleans as a complete cultural landscape. Yes, the Garden District and Uptown of the crescent has returned we are assured, but where will the Stanley Kowalskis or the King Olivers live? Where will the cultural creative tension born of the total social order come to reside? Will jazz, rhythm 'n' blues, and the heart of Mardi Gras become ossified relics of a wild and wicked past? We know the distinctive cuisine will be maintained, in the recipes and high-ground tourist restaurants at least, but what of the juke joints and the neighborhoods of shotgun and raised cottages in which these cultural treasures were conceived, nurtured, and housed?

The life and soul of the city is certainly tied in the imagination to the mental health of the rest of the nation. For many observers, it is obvious that the situation in New Orleans represents a test of our national will. It is clear who are most fully affected, and lo and behold they are the very people who were lied about in the media, who were displaced most severely, and whose grandmothers, uncles, children, and pets were swept away when the levees broke and Lake Pontchartrain spilled over into town. These are the neighborhoods the tourist guidebooks mostly *did not* recommend for visiting, even during Mardi Gras.

What we fear is the death of the spirit along with Mardi Gras in the rest of town, the celebration of cultural vitality that has resided in neighborhood beneficial and recreational societies that emerges not only before Lent, but whenever a death provokes the march to the cemetery and back—a jazz funeral. This vernacular celebration that is tied not so much to European as to Caribbean festivities, this time of year that replays all those earlier times in which the good times rolled (though not always on paved streets). What we fear even more is the disappearance or scattering of the African American residents who created these other Mardi Gras, and are essential to the spirit of the city and the rest of the country.

This book connects the histories and cultures of Mardi Gras, the Gulf Coast, and the Caribbean to give body to what we see as the potential impact of misconceiving the rebuilding process. It is an altogether chancy, combative, and transgressive story worthy of the risky city-in-spite-of-itself—a city built on constant invention and reinvention, one that has woven its way into the dreamlife of the rest of America and beyond: a city that boasts of Mardi Gras and the cultural interactions and conflicts that traverse almost three centuries. In this we follow the spirit of Duke Ellington's laments in his last great composition, *New Orleans Suite* (1970). The opening piece of that work, "Blues for New Orleans," uncharacteristically mixes the sonorities of a church organ with a walking-paced melody line, and so richly evokes the poignant complexities of the city and its musics that it seemed to us the best allusion to embody what we want to get at in words.

Here, we want to record the multiple travesties, the openly imitational and often phantasmagoric interfaces between an assortment of folk that produced and reproduced such a place, such a way of being, such a "Land of Dreams" according to the lyrics romantic return in "Basin Street Blues" (1926). We are reminded also of the words of Kenneth Bilby, one of the most tireless observers of the culture of African American communities: "The flow of styles in the Atlantic world is even more dynamic than the movement of people. It is not always easy to distinguish cultural parallels that arose independently from those that stem from migration and diffusion." Clearly both kinds have played a role in the cultural and musical development of what may be called Greater Afro-America. We approach New Orleans as a creole construction, a culture consisting of artistically assembled elements of several Old World cultures made new.

New Orleans emerged like an Atlantis from under the sea (and from under the Mississippi River and Lake Pontchartrain). It was the city in which some of the most important American arts were born. The creole creativity of the place turned America on its ear, eye, and tongue with jazz—music made of old parts and put together in utterly new ways; architecture that commingled Norman rooflines, West African floor plans, and native materials of mud and moss; food that simmered in French sauces (court bouillon) Spanish stews (jambalaya and caldo), African ingredients and sensibilities (okra and deep fried), and Native American delicacies (sassafras and crawfish.).

Conserving styles from a multitude of Old Worlds—from west, central, and southern Africa, from many strains of Europe, including Spain, France, Scotland, and their New World outcomes in Cuba, Mexico, and Canada (especially Quebec and the Maritime Acadian areas)—New Orleans culture provides a new stylistic synthesis each generation, a new creation in which recognizable parts and processes coexist despite entrenched social and racial hierarchies. This city is a vernacular society and a culture of cityscape, founded on Latinate libertine populism leavened with African styled performances, many of which years ago were reinterpreted into new forms such as jazz and rhythm 'n' blues, soul and funk, beloved around the world—all overlayered with colonial decadence and decay, conjoined to the quirks and intolerances of the American South.

The decentering hurricane revealed not only weak levees and poor evacuation planning, but also huge ruptures in the social structure along lines of race and class, as well as unequal access to resources and a growing debate over who deserved to be kept from returning to the city. Katrina's flood forced us to think about what a new cityscape might look like without the very neighborhoods that are the soul and source of much New Orleans music, food, fashion, religion, and building arts. How could one parade for Mardi Gras if neighborhoods of shotgun houses, Creole cottages, camelbacks, and the like lay silent in ruins; or with neighborhood bars and dancehalls closed, no relatives in sight, no friends and no enemies to see or be seen for the carnivalesque purposes of showing off to and showing up one's intimate colleagues and combatants?

Journalists such as Joel Garreau of the *Washington Post* have argued for a laissez faire approach to New Orleans, suggesting that the city will still have its famed French Quarter, its American business, its Uptown residential sectors, its port, its oil industry, and, most debatably, its tourism economy restored intact. Cultural workers know this fallacy, as these are merely the most visible assets of a city that has the most African and Mediterranean (albeit creolized) sensibilities of any urban center in North America. What such writers fail to notice is what will become of the people who work, who sweep up, who wipe babies and put them to bed, who have crafted the small, but often stylish dwellings in the neighborhoods they call home and have plastered and painted the big houses of Uptown and Garden district residents.

The United States needs the Crescent City for many economic reasons, but also as a symbol of cultural freedoms, worked out in pain and pleasure and expressed in a shared but distinctive series of ways among peoples from Europe, Africa, and Native America who have called themselves New Orleanians for almost three centuries. In some ways New Orleans has served the public imagination, both in the city and outside it, as a democratically diverse, creative, and romantically reactionary distillation of the American soul. Most important, and least recognized by those visiting for just a few days and writing about the experience on the travel page of their local paper, is that New Orleans is the contact point for introducing stylistic alternatives born in the Afro-Latin Caribbean and places even farther east.

The Gulf South has provided alternative ways of thinking about almost everything in American life. New Orleans' parade of peoples and cultures, its principal attractions to immigrants and tourists, reveals an enduring concoction of styles beyond the waspish perspectives of those who have not yet gotten caught "the flash of the spirit," as Robert Farris Thompson phrased it years ago. This city is a world monument to living culture, to the diverse underclass's ability to create sounds and styles of performative and material art now spread across the world. To avoid helping find new ways to rebuild old neighborhoods or to fail to carry forward the culture of communities, we must accept that among the most revered places and shapes of human expression in America and the globe will be left as a toxic shambles for an underclass without the financial assets and political power to stop the bulldozers. The lack of a proactive plan to rebuild the wooden cityscape suggests that the future New Orleans will be more for gazing by outsiders than living by natives.

This is a future we refuse to accept, and for this reason we turn to the city's most elegant and electric, protean and pervasive, comforting and disquieting moment: Mardi Gras. Traveling back and forth through time, scoping north, south, east, and west, parading up and down the streets, and watching with delight from the crowd, we offer a wide-ranging look at Mardi Gras culture from a multitude of angles. We make take some seemingly strange turns, such as our discussions of baseball or flea markets or garbage disposal, but it always brings us back to the same point: we hope to see Mardi Gras and the creative power of carnival resurrected and re-formed once again—and with it a new New Orleans made.

*   *   *

For the past forty years, our work has focused on how order arises out of disorder, an approach that goes well beyond the argument that African American culture is merely a set of survival techniques created by enslaved people to operate beyond the reach of the slaveholder and his representatives. We see these developments of the New World as more than a set of hidden agendas for resistance on the part of slaves. Even under the system of enslavement, new manufacturing and trade techniques created opportunities for the celebration of life forces, African style. The slaves themselves seized the moment of regular celebrations and developed them into slave holidays. And later, after slavery was ended, the same holiday times became occasions for the celebration of emancipation. Before and after Katrina's winds and flood, we are faced with evidence of a set of adaptive and inventive techniques of celebration whereby men and women made something out of what had seemed to others to be nothing. (We're reminded of poet Derek Walcott's retort to V. S. Naipaul's charge that nothing had ever been created in the West Indies. Walcott said, "Nothing will always be created in the West Indies . . . because what will come out of there is like nothing one has ever seen.")

The project of our combined scholarship—observing the performed life and the records kept of older historical moments—began with a decision to resist easy explanations that assumed that the enslaved Africans lost all of their cultures as a result of the Middle Passage and the experience of plantation life. Rather, we have sought to find the voices and bodies of those who resisted artfully and soulfully: the slaves as well as the planters and overseers who found themselves mirroring each other as they learned to live under the conditions created by the new agricultural practices of the plantation. If they lived uneasily with each other, they were bound together by the mirror effect. This was a complex social and cultural arrangement, one that involved the family in the Big House and the lowliest of field slaves under the surveillance of an overseer, as well as the workers in the field, the maritime and riverine slaves, the market hagglers, the secret healers and the open dealers. Everybody was under surveillance, not only the slaves, and together they saw all. Our ethnographic and historical observations and our reading of the works of earlier observers made us aware of an America altogether different from that imagined by those seeing these continents as mere outposts of European Enlightenment or proto-industrial evolution. Quite the contrary, we saw a world of vibrant inventions, but not one driven by "enlightenment" or "civility." We discerned a social experiment altogether less scientific, more reckless and restless. In fact, it was an experiment in spite of itself, the result of arcadian dreamwork of adventurers with the ear of the monarch and a hand in the pocket of the wealthy who had some venture capital lying around and the availability of enslaved workers from the interior of West and Central Africa. For here in the New World, these outposts consisted of peoples from throughout the Old World who were engaged in some of the earliest experiments in capitalist economies.

For many years, in fact since the mid-1960s when we first entered into this conversation, we have attempted to direct attention to what Robert Farris Thompson was calling "The Black Atlantic" and John Szwed and Roger Abrahams were regarding as cultural formations emerging "after Africa" or in "the Greater Caribbean." Nick Spitzer was an early entrant into this discussion, a public folklorist employed in encouraging communities to build on the cultural riches found throughout this region, and bringing attention to wider publics the art forms emerging from the embers as the plantation system came to an end throughout this region. Inevitably, we found ourselves especially taken by the story that emerged of the ways in which the whole Creole World developed, a world anchored by the major ports of call throughout the Americas: not only New Orleans and the Gulf Coast ports in general, but Port au Prince and Port-of-Spain, Savannah and Charleston, Havana and Santo Domingo, Kingston and Belize, the many other smaller ports in the Lesser Antilles, the Anglophonic, Lusiphonic, and Francophonic outposts, and even some of the smaller towns that have maintained local cultural variations on the same Creole pattern

Our goal then, as now, was to call attention to the mixture of stylistic traits found throughout that large geographic area in which slaves came together with a set of would-be rational entrepreneur planters, too many of whom left the plantations to managers from the scoundrel class. The competing and interacting cultures of these various groups developed from the public moments of New Orleans into what they are today, and their future and reinvention is only secure if their history—its complexities and elasticity during the past three centuries—can be imagined again.

By using evidence derived from all the senses as they occur in dance, music, taste, and smell, we sought out the common features of cultural forms extending beyond the usual disciplinary divisions between script and print, between music, visual arts, dance, religious and healing practices. Our interests consistently centered on the vernacular forms that arose in now one port of call, now another, forms that were soon shared throughout the region—indeed throughout the world.

Of course, the amazing confrontations and commingling of cultures in New Orleans repeatedly seemed to be among the best test cases of how varied peoples and cultures crafted creative ways of interacting at the boundaries between peoples in neighborhoods. Given the reminders of Africa that manifested themselves at Congo Square and other open gathering places in the emerging trade center, the response of the planters and traders representing European authorities is difficult to read. In a sense, they were busy opening trade routes and developing natural resources into "raw materials" to be refined once they were transshipped. They created a world of middlemen, factors of the products of rational agriculture in this new setting, agents who sought to cement commercial relations. This called for the creation of a rigid hierarchy in which classes were established in terms of where one was involved in the production process. Yet the class system of the Old World did not necessarily map onto the realities of the New World. The new market economy elevated those "in trade" to the point where commercially adept and upward striving people might afford to emulate their betters.

Moreover, questions abounded in this new geographical environment. How would the activities of the public sphere in European cities, essentially bourgeois in origin, be adapted to the new kinds of towns and cities being assembled in such strange places in the New

World? How could the establishment defend good manners and decorum in these outposts and maintain the sense of fun and freedom made possible in the new mercantile economy? Playing could hardly be carried out in public when there were so many possible observers and imitators from other cultures out there. Yet the tropicality of New Orleans demanded a good deal of outdoor socializing in public places. Could Old World democratizing proclivities be transferable to the Gulf Coast so easily? Isn't that the strange double feature of New Orleans life, the juxtaposition of the genteel with the outrageous, the elite white Krewe of Comus and the elite black Zulu parade. Such genteel behavior—"good manners" if you will—were far from a given in their European homes now left behind. They had been achieved at the expense of the suppression of natural desires: at the table, in the withdrawing room, in court, and the many other places where civil behavior was on show.

New Orleans and other New World outposts seemed to provide an interesting test. Would those who distanced themselves from the metropolitan centers be able to maintain the suppression of sensual gratification in the name of civility? Or would they be seduced to the old disorders, and yes, sloppiness and behavior labeled immoral?

In Mardi Gras, we encounter the deepest of profane play being held between the most sacred season of the Christian year, starting with Christmas and ending with Easter. It is a frenzy of consumption that produces a mountain of trash, where even the throwaways, the beads and doubloons tossed to the crowds as souvenirs, are trashy, too. Deep trash and deep play beget a kind of dark secrecy that plays against the open revelry of the event itself.

We follow folklorist Dan Crowley in these matters, the only scholar among us who can claim to have died at Carnival. Intrepid in his wheelchair, he went year in and year out. As he put it:

Profanation is the specialty of European Carnivals, elements of which are specifically designed to be sacrilegious, as shocking as possible to the conservative and the religious. But in the New World Carnivals, such specific sacrilege is rather rare, and where it occurs it is a specialty of the upper classes who are usually relatively lighter-skinned than their lower-class countryman. Bahians and African-nationalist Cariocas (natives of Rio) often compare their increasingly race-conscious Afoxé and Bloco Afro parading organizations with Catholic religious street processions on Corpus Christi and other holy days. "This is our chance to display our culture and religious beliefs, just like the [white] Catholics of their festivals. . . . That's why they are down on Carnival, always trying to stop it or change it or limit it." For people of this orientation, coming out in Carnival is a political act as well as a cultural one.

Long before Crowley, visitors to New Orleans and Mardi Gras noticed the intersection of many cultures. When journalist, folklorist, and early Afro-Americanist Lafcadio Hearn left New Orleans for the Caribbean in the late nineteenth century, eventually to write *Two Years in the French West Indies* (1889), he found cultural similarities between the two places everywhere he looked: the elaborate masked bands of pre-Lenten carnival, work songs in the cane fields, the calinda dance, the practice of vodun ceremonies, songs of derision and praise, all in the French Creole language. This came as no surprise to Hearn, for he had already published *Gombo Zhebes* (gumbo with herbs or vegetables, but not fish or fowl, as consumed on Maundy Thursday) in 1885, a small and charming collection of proverbs from six black French Creole-speaking parts of the world. If Hearn had not gone on to seek a radically different exoticism in Japan, he might have lived to see yet other cultural parallels, such as French folk tunes played on the accordion changed into zydeco music by black Creoles of rural Louisiana, and in turn into meringue in Haiti and into the biguine in Martinique; or he might have heard the development of polyphonic dance bands in both New Orleans and St. Pierre, Martinique.

Hearn arrived in Martinique in 1887 as the city faced a calamity: a smallpox epidemic that was ravaging the French island. Yet the people of St. Pierre unflinchingly incorporated the pestilence into their carnival:

Extraordinary things are happening in the streets through which the procession passes. Pest-smitten women rise from their beds to costume themselves—to mask face[s] already made unrecognizable by the hideous malady—and stagger out to join the dancers. . . . [I]n the Rue Ste.-Marthe there are three young girls sick with the disease, who hear the blowing of the horns and the pattering of feet and clapping of hands in chorus—they get up to look through the slats of their windows on the masquerade and the creole passion of the dance comes upon them. "Ah!" cries one . . . "We will have our fill of fun—what matter if we die after!" And all mask, and join the rout, and dance down to the Savane, and over the river-bridge into the high streets of the Fort, carrying contagion with them!

Even in the midst of the pandemic horror, not only did the carnival go on, but the people compelled their circumstances to submit to their celebration, their dance, and their music. Such it was in 1887, and such it may be after the rage of Hurricane Katrina and the ineptitude of so many politicians.

*   *   *

Originally the capital of French Louisiana, New Orleans was ceded to the Spanish in 1764 and remained under Spanish influence until France reacquired it in 1800 and sold its claim to the United States in 1803. During this period the French and Spanish islands of the Caribbean were the main sources of slaves for the Louisiana area, with thousands of additional slaves arriving from Saint-Domingue following the slave rebellion which drove many of their former masters and free people of color (*gens de couleur libres*) to North America directly or via Cuba. The cultural connections between Africa, Spain, and France, along with parallels to the Caribbean, were thus renewed, complicated, and (re)creolized in early nineteenth-century New Orleans.

The impact of French culture on the music of the Americas, like its influence on other aspects of culture, is not as easily viewed as the affects of England, Spain, or even Portugal. Part of the reason for this oversight is that France's territorial holdings in the New World have shrunk to only a few outposts in modern times: now all that remains are the islands of St. Pierre and Miquelon in the St. Lawrence on the eastern shore of Canada near the Province of Québec; Martinique and Guadeloupe in the Caribbean; and Guyane (French Guiana) on the north coast of South America. But recognized or not, French influence has been considerable and enduring, especially in the West Indies. France remained a force in Haiti long after the Revolution of 1791 had forced it to cede control. And many of the islands now identified with the British—Grenada, St. Kitts, St. Lucia, Trinidad, Dominica, St. Vincent—were colonized, in whole or in part, by the French. In the United States, the former Louisiana Territory still shows the marks of French control: the state of Louisiana is officially bilingual (though they haven't agreed on what the approved form of French will be), the Napoleonic Code remains the basis for state law, and New Orleans' houses, streets, and squares reflect eighteenth-century planning. The locus of Francité in Louisiana remains in the Acadian or Cajun parishes of rural south and southwestern Louisiana, where Catholicism, the French language, local Mardi Gras, and Cajun music and Creole zydeco carry on and flourish in many communities.

France's musical contribution to the West Indies includes a body of eighteenth- and nineteenth-century dances (the quadrille, mazurka, waltz, and contradance) that are all popular in other spheres of influence, and, like the schottische or polka, are associated with one European country or another. The French also brought a full range of musical instruments and performance techniques to the New World, as well as a folk song tradition, brass and string bands, the occasions for their music (Roman Catholic holidays and feasts, theatrical events, folk dramas, and parties). They also provided (and enforced) a social structure based on subtle gradations of color that gave rise to specialized music and musicians to serve different segments of the population. In this color-coded playworld, images of both Africans and Indians held a special role, calling attention to these Mardi Gras Indian performers as wild men and fearless warrior-dancers in dazzling feathers and beads, or clowns in motley rags.

The quadrille, important in both the Old World and the New, is of special interest because it was known internationally as a dance favored at the courts of many European monarchs. Dances by the same name in the New World tended to take on local variations, and when combined with African-styled rhythms they became signature dances in a number of island communities, not all of them French. And quite often these very dances play out the motives of black/white conflictive interaction in strangely inflected ways.

When we turn to Africa's contribution to the French-speaking West Indies, it is difficult to be precise about cultural sources. For one thing, records of slavery are inadequate for this purpose. We do know that Haiti (then Saint-Domingue, which included the present-day Dominican Republic) and Guadeloupe both drew slaves in roughly equal numbers from West Africa and Angola, plus other areas, while Martinique and Guyane favored slaves from West Africa. And from aural evidence (supported by travelers' and slavers' accounts) it now appears that the influence of Kongo-Angolan cultures (from what are now the People's Republic of Angola and the Democratic Republic of Congo) were dominant in the African music of the French West Indies. This is apparent in drum and other instrument types and styles of playing, in dance postures and names of dances, and in the events the music accompanied, such as stick dancing and ritual combat. In addition, there are the general characteristics of West and Central African musics: call-and-response, multiple meters, and vocal role-switching.

In any case, Franco-African cultural interaction has created a variety of forms that weave themselves across the fabric of French New World societies. In New Orleans the French impact on early jazz goes well beyond the French Opera House that protean jazz pianist Jelly Roll Morton lauded on Alan Lomax's recordings: to the larger creative tensions between French, Spanish, African, and African American cultures and players who bring jazz to its beginning point, where street parade and parlor sensibilities collide and cotillion courtship rituals mime European style while Congo Square's dance and drum sessions lean more toward Africa. Jazz in all its variations has been influenced by French musicians such as Louis Moreau Gottschalk and the musical pedagogy of nuns, just as surely as by the carriers of complex rhythm patterns of West African and Caribbean ceremonies and by the blue tonalities and transformed spirituals of African Americans.

Yet, after all this, searching after indisputable sources of West Indian music or dance or festive costuming is difficult, even if tempting, Consider the complicated case of the Masqueraders, a group of dancers from Gingerland Parish on Nevis in the West Indies, who perform a set of dances featuring the quadrille and the reel or contradance. By legend, these dances were learned from itinerant French dancemasters, some of whom had learned the technique. They passed through the islands in the eighteenth century, when Nevis was the spa of choice for the region, and some of the sets they dance continue to have French calls to them. But, before they take their show to Charlestown or Basse-Terre, these dancers perform from yard to yard in the luck-visit style of countryside England and Ireland. They alternate with other groups who enact "St. George and the Turk," or "Shakespeare Lessons" (scenes from *Richard II* and *Julius Caesar*), or who are dressed in black cutaways (the "Buzzards," a name also found for such groups in New Orleans). Many of these groups of "sporty fellows" continue to borrow from nineteenth-century blackface minstrelsy and use their high-toned get-up as a way of pulling off some vaudeville routines.

The Masqueraders themselves dress in a motley array of high contrast colored cloth, with bells on their ankles and a stylized tomahawk and a ring of peacock plumes on their heads. It is an outfit that would be equally at home in the English Morris dance or the Italian *commedia dell'arte*, as well as in many African agricultural rituals or among royal pageantry. On Nevis and St. Kitts, both British mother colonies founded in the 1620s, there are still many different groups of countryside revelers that play on the historic enmity between black slaves and white slavers, often in blackface or painted red, yet dancing a send-up of the ways of the planters. One of the plays, in fact, pits one of the founding families of Nevis and St. Kitts, the Warners, against out of control "bulls" who continually rush at the bystanders and scare the children. Another group of sporty fellows, "Cowboys and Indians," make bragging speeches learned from pulp novels and movies from the United States. The point of it all emerges as the two groups have a battle, with speeches in which they pledge death to the others, and the Indians proclaim "The Black Man must live and the White Man must die."

Tellingly, a casual reference to a deep historical reality sneaks into the midst of an entertainment that has almost nothing to do with black/white relations. Dan Crowley was right when he suggested that in every one of the carnivals that he observed (and there were a great many), none of the Mardi Gras celebrations attempted to hide the racial face-off between elites and grassroots neighborhoods. He added that the blacker the population, the greater the number of references taken from African aesthetic resources. In the same vein, anthropologist Morton Marks argues that the deeper into the festival experience, the greater the number of African-derived cultural features come to the surface in the music and dance.

Following Crowley and Marks, we are tempted to another grand aesthetic claim: there are no festivals in the Gulf South or the Caribbean that fail to articulate the continuing divisions between whites and blacks, however gradated and creolized. All the Carnivals arise, historically, from the celebration of two different, albeit intersecting, holiday celebrations: one stemming from European power display techniques, and using costumes and floats derived from medieval tournaments and Renaissance masques; and another that emerges from the slaves' holidays and continue to draw on the contestive spirit and elegance of the Transatlantic Black World. A third element is joined when indigenous Indian practices relating to life passage events are taken into account. That the different styles of display and celebration encounter each other each year on the streets of these cities is testimony to a history of creative improvizations and accommodations. The processes formed and reformed one another and took place amid the broader process of creolization, perhaps the oldest conception of social change known in the Americas.

Strange Mergers and Deep Mixture Making

It is impossible to comprehend Mardi Gras or New Orleans or, for that matter, the Americas, without confronting the concept of creolization. "Creole" is an adjective and a noun heard throughout Louisiana and the Gulf Coast, and it is widely associated elsewhere with that region through movies, advertising, and tourism. But the term has a much older and wider application. "Creole" historically meant someone born in the New World, and in Louisiana it could refer to the offspring of French planters as well as the children of newly arrived slaves. Creole has also come to mean something entirely new, or a surprising mixture of ingredients, and can be applied to a style of cuisine, to music, clothing, architecture, literature, language, to a mode of behavior, or to a person of a certain color or social status. It has been said to be an impure state of being, but also the purest state possible.

As a social process, scholars and politicians have taken to calling creolization a way in which things or people of historically unrelated backgrounds and history come into contact and change over time. Creolization is an especially useful way of thinking about performance forms, especially language and music in the West Indies, where the process and the term itself have been operating continuously for more than three hundred years.

The development of language in the Greater Caribbean demonstrates a wide array of cultural interactions and conflicts, and many linguists have been fascinated and troubled by the existence of related creole languages that are connected by common elements of grammar and syntax. Yet, these languages also share some features of

European languages. In areas that were politically dominated by France, for example, the surface features of talk bear a sufficient amount of French that for many years it was regarded simply as a regional dialect. Yet, like music and dance and other sorts of display activities, a more complex, interesting, and in fact comprehensible process is at work.

Creole languages are often called broken, bastardized, or mixed-up and corrupted versions of standard European languages. And if thought of as no more than words on a list written in a European writing system—as they are usually represented—they do appear to be strangely, even comically, European. But linguists tell us that when put into use in speech these words show principles of organization that owe little to European language history. Rather than seeing them as faulty and contaminated dialects of European languages, we might better think of West Indian creoles as converged, reassembled, "Africanized" languages, products of the joining together of two or more historically distinct languages under the very pressurized circumstances of colonization and slavery. Even though many features of creoles can be found in some Western European language or other, they are not found in the same combinations as seen in the West Indies. To put the consequences of all this bluntly, a Parisian suddenly dropped into the Haitian hills would neither understand nor be completely understood by monolingual French Creole speakers.

Creole languages took different forms in different colonies, and the most variable feature was the lexicon drawn upon. In French colonies, the vocabulary was borrowed in good part from French, and in English colonies English words predominated as sources. A third form of this creole, Papiamento, is found among the islands with a strong Portuguese and Dutch contingent (a language still employed in Aruba, Bonaire, and Curaçao). Given the importance of New Orleans as a center of trade, all these ways of speaking once coexisted there, with French Creole serving as the lingua franca, more or less understood (if not spoken) by virtually everyone.

Those who didn't speak French Creole as their everyday language tended to call it "patois," a word with negative connotations. Patois is the word now used in Anglophonic areas, with similar feelings that it is a broken language. It may be the primary language of the "underclass," the poor, and the stigmatized, but it has its own virtues and functions for all segments of the population. Typically, it serves as the language of emotions, of love, pain, and humor. In Martinique, even Standard French speakers sometimes end their jokes with Creole punchlines, talk affectionately in it, and curse in it. It's no surprise, then, that most of the popular music in the French West Indies is sung in Creole.

In New Orleans, neighborhoods with a distinctly continental cast existed alongside ones where the West Indian creole people, who did not come from France but from one or another island in the Francophonic areas of the Greater Caribbean and spoke French. In every area of the French Caribbean, for example, Standard French is considered to be the local standard language. Yet by no means is it spoken or understood by everyone. In fact, the areas where Acadians originally settled in the Eastern Maritime provinces of Canada, beyond the more metropole-oriented Québec region, another kind of French was also spoken, one that also found its detractors among the French elite.

The relexification from African to Creole language formations is commonly described by focusing on the most volatile and labile level of the language—lexicon. New words keep emerging at the center of the discourse on black performance, generated from within. But as often as not they are terms like jamming, breaking, cutting, rapping, and other words that become key words in one generation of creative artists and exegetes and are replaced by the next generation. When we speak with one generation about, say, "playing the dozens," for a couple of decades young people would say. "Oh, you mean . . . ," then use words that are the latest versions of the same thing. If the point is pushed as to whether playing the dozens is understandable to them, they often reply, "that's old" or "that's what my father or grandfather used to say." Such words are part of the receptive competence of the speakers, but not central to their talk. Then, by the next generation, the old terms are as likely as not to be recycled back into use.

This lamination together of words for talk, and for talk about talk, is always there, even if the entire range of terms is not used by one generation or another. The older word "signifying"—meaning a kind of indirect joking around about personal relationships—is no longer heard as often as terms such as cracking or snapping, but these new words never totally replace signifying, which after all has been around for ten generations.

These shifts and changes would be problems if we were faced only with changes in the key terms of the vocabulary. But the process of word substitution is somewhat analogous with what takes place as new musical forms, new dances, new song-types come on the scene. These events, whether shifts in language or dancing or music, can be and are read through symbolic places in time and space. What this amounts to is a universe of individuals carrying out creative research on the vernacular level, which relexifies across time periods and across linguistic and cultural boundaries. Words and phrases are constantly borrowed from contiguous times and peoples. The argument could be made that the same is happening constantly in musical style and dance fads.

A gesture that seems to demonstrate the importance of this type of interpretation comes from baseball. With the introduction of so many Creole ballplayers into major league baseball, a lot of new gestures have been introduced that, when they first arose, seemed like show-boating and nothing more—like the little hop Sammy Sosa introduced into his batting style to indicate that he knows that he has hit a home run. It seemed idiosyncratic on his part until spectators were forced to notice that Sosa wasn't the only player doing this. A lot of other Latino players did it, too, especially those who, like Sosa, come from the Dominican Republic, indeed mostly from one town, San Pedro de Macquaries.

But seemingly even deeper is the gesture a great many African American players—Dominican, Venezuelan, Californian—have introduced in the recent past. After making a hit, the player gets to the base, claps once, looks upward, raises his right hand, and points to the sky, usually with the index figure as the pointer and the rest of the hand simply in support, with the fingers curled. This sort of gesture might be taken as showboating—just a bit too much for those from a baseball culture in which players are supposed to be undemonstrative after getting a hit, especially a home run. But to those who come from such a repressed tradition, the gesture seems related to the Roman Catholic beliefs of Latin American players. After all, they cross themselves when they come up to hit. Thus, when it began to be introduced into the batters' routines, it seemed like the players were making some kind of claim about their close relationship to God, as they put it, "from the hands to God."

This kind of discussion about language seems too simple if one approaches the region in terms of the entire range of expressive resources shared from one enclave to the next. Something like relexification certainly has occurred, then, but not only with regard to ways of speaking. The higher intensity moments of shared experience provided by singing and dancing, marching and working together, give us a model of development that reveals new layers of constant cultural adaptation and borrowings throughout the region. In New Orleans, the creolization process extends to virtually all aspects of culture, and the local variation serves as a signature of the region. Couple this with the establishment of urban zones known for their sensual pleasures, and you begin to see the uniqueness of the city. In such a case, the relexification of languages, musics, dances, foods and drinks, and vernacular traditions of craftwork in house construction came together at the mouth of the Mississippi. But the term relexification doesn't suggest the fuller story; creolization is a better way to understand New Orleans and Mardi Gras, for it suggests a comprehensive and dynamic phenomenon of cultural give and take, invention and reinvention, of dialogue and disagreement.

Otherwise secret or hidden ways can be the most easily adaptable traditions, because they occur in public. In fact, they constitute the public on these occasions. They translate nicely and with the appropriate frissons already built in that will attract the attention of the traveler—as they are often described in the historical travel accounts—and the tourist, who are fed the local legends that can then be repeated. More, these touristic entertainments have all the elements of play: risk, chance, imitational travesty making, contained conflicts and contests, and are often translated into dance forms that invite participation, thus upsetting the rules of everyday segregated life.

The Spanish Tinge, Second-Line, and the Black Atlantic Origins of Jazz

While the sources of similarities between the musics of New Orleans, rural Louisiana, Martinique, Guadeloupe, Haiti, and French Guiana may seem obvious to close listeners, the reciprocal influences between Cuban and Afro-French music are not so apparent. But even a listen to their musical interactions uncovers an astounding amount of cultural ingenuity and confluence as cultures, musicians, and rhythms came together. While one can trace the sources of certain instruments, instrumental ensembles, and stylistic techniques, the music enacted defies easy classification. When the music is played, its sources are subordinated to its overall sound. The complexity of the borrowings and the rapidity of the adaptations are perhaps the clearest examples of how complicated the process of creolization can become for those in search for cultural origins and influence. It seems as if the recent development of what is called World Music was prefigured and probably grew out of the festive and club musics of the Black Atlantic. What may appear to be only a recent intermingling of these elements has more likely been a process going on for hundreds of years.

Jelly Roll Morton, a composer and pianist born and raised in the cultural hothouse of fin-de-siècle New Orleans, was the first person to underscore the importance of other musics of the New World for understanding American jazz and popular music. Seated with folklorist Alan Lomax before a recording machine in Coolidge Auditorium in the Library of Congress in 1938, he remarked that one of the elements that distinguished jazz from ragtime was the presence of the

"Spanish tinge," what some call the *habanera*, or the "tango bass line." What he saw as a basic part of American music, later commentators dismissed as an imported craze; the music he thought called for a pan-American comparative perspective, they treated as an accidental and limited convergence of American and exotic forms. But Morton was more right than wrong.

The Spanish tinge can be found in a number of popular American dances of some seventy years ago, such as the slow drag or the Congo grind. New Orleans Drummer Baby Dodds said that in the first decade of the 1900s the blues were played "very, very slow, and not like today, but in a Spanish rhythm," and a number of popular tunes of the early 1900's were built entirely on this tango-like bass line: "Panama," "Charleston," "Dardanella," "Spanish Dreams," and especially Jelly Roll Morton's own "The Crave," "Creepy Feeling," "Spanish Swat," "Fickle Fay Creep," and "'Mamanita.''

But "Spanish" seems to be too specific a term to locate these rhythm and musical patterns. Underlying Morton's Spanish tinge, whether in a bass line or in the accenting of a melody line, was an uneven rhythm pattern characteristic of Sub-Saharan Africa and perhaps all the musics of the black diaspora—what Ghanaian ethnomusicologist J. H. Kwabena Nketia calls additive rhythm (as opposed to the even units typical of European rhythms). Some refer to the African additive rhythm pattern as 3-3-2 or some combination of those numbers, meaning the grouping of beats and the accents given to them. This Spanish-African tinge can be found in ragtime composer Scott Joplin's 1909 "Solace—A Mexican Serenade," in the introduction to W. C. Handy's "St. Louis Blues," in the phrasing of some blues and gospel songs, but also in the left-hand parts of some stride pianists such as James P. Johnson in his "Keep Off the Mardi Grass" and in the piano parts of King Oliver's Creole Jazz Band's recordings of "Weatherbird Rag" and "Snake Rag." But it also occurs in other musics than jazz and in areas far from New Orleans, and is not specifically Spanish or even Latin: it is also found in New World areas colonized by the Portuguese and the English, and, if anything, more often in the French territories. Lafcadio Hearn, for instance, wrote down a "habanera" rhythm he heard in Martinique in the 1880s. Since then many others have found it all across the Americas—in Cuba, the Dominican Republic, Puerto Rico, Haiti, Mexico, Argentina, and Brazil.

It's not surprising that Morton, a New Orleanian, should be sensitive to such connections. Nowhere else has this rhythm pattern persisted more strongly than in the Crescent City, where for several centuries outdoor band tradition has brought together European military and folk band music with the wind and drum orchestra traditions of Sub-Saharan Africa. New Orleans was where jazz drummers like Baby Dodds fused elements of African stick and hand drum patterns with the martial drum rudiments of Western Europe; and where the special rhythmic characteristics of vernacular music allowed contemporary Latin American musical influences to reunite with jazz and rhythm 'n' blues. It is this rhythm and the habanera bass line which is at the heart of the famous New Orleans "second line" beat, a pattern so widely shared by New Orleanians that it constitutes the center of that city's tradition of celebration.

In the New Orleans Mardi Gras, as in many of the Caribbean and Latin American street parades, no clear division can be drawn between those in the parade and its spectators. Paraders drift in and out of line, stopping to talk to others or to take a break, sometimes being left behind only to catch up several blocks later. Following the bands—called the first-line—there are crowds of people who dance and strut in their own individual fashion and who are not members of the first group, but are what is called the second-line. No facet of Mardi Gras and tradition in New Orleans sets them off from European street celebrations more than this self-organized ragtag group.

Film writer and New Orleans acolyte Michael Goodwin once attempted to ferret out the meanings of second-line in an essay he wrote for the *Village Voice* on New Orleans parades and street bands.

He concluded that second-line was a gathering that danced joyfully behind any parade, but in doing so also reminded us of the funeral parade's refusal to accept death as the end of anything. Second-line was also a set of loosely coordinated steps the dancers do as part of a strut behind the band, twirling and pumping umbrellas in the air and waving handkerchiefs. It is a dance that perhaps recalled the African gatherings in Congo Square that had been forbidden many years ago because their collective force and potential had frightened whites. Second-line was also a style perfected by New Orleans drummers. But it might also be, Goodwin added, "a central mystery, a shared secret through which New Orleanians celebrate their African origins, power culture, self-knowledge."

Once, when asked to explain second-line rhythm, Dr. John (Mac Rebennack, the New Orleans pianist and singer) suggested that it was similar to Latin rhythms. The difference lay in the syncopation created by New Orleans bass drummers playing "double-clutch rhythms, like two eighth-notes rather than one quarter-note as a pickup or as a basic pulsation. . . . you get a feeling like da-doom, da-doom, da-doom, da-doom-doom-doom/da-doom, da-doom, da-doom-doom-doom." Instead of using the cymbals to keep the beat, as in jazz, second-line drumming establishes the rhythm by the bass drum, with two-handed snare drum playing, and the high-hat cymbals striking on the back-beat. New Orleans guitarist Danny Barker recalled Black Benny, a drummer from his youth, this way: "He had an African beat . . . he could move a whole band with just that bass drum." (Dizzy Gillespie also drew attention to the importance of the bass drum when he once said of a marching band in South Carolina that its rhythms were similar to those of "comparsa," the street carnival music of Cuba. Dr. John has even spoken of a link between second-line and the samba of Brazil.)

The traditions of New Orleans neighborhoods keep many local forms alive, and second-line rhythm permeates all forms of New

Orleans vernacular music. This beat, in its various permutations, can be heard on New Orleans rhythm & blues recordings from the late 1940s forward, such as Professor Longhair's "Mardi Gras in New Orleans," Barbara George's 1961 "I Know," James Wayne's "Junco Partner," Prince La La's "She Put the Hurt on Me," and on jazz recordings such as Ahmad Jamal's early versions of "Poinciana" (where the rhythm section includes former New Orleans parade drummer Vernell Fournier) and the Dirty Dozen's "Caravan." Even avant-garde jazz drummers from New Orleans—such as Ed Blackwell, a key member of the Ornette Coleman Quartet—typically focus most of their playing on the snare drum.

On the question of the origins of jazz, New Orleans has many parallels with other French areas, especially Martinique and Guadeloupe. These two clusters of islands are located among the Windward Islands of the Lesser Antilles, separated from each other by the British dependency of Dominica, itself a former French colony. Both Martinique and Guadeloupe have been more or less continuously colonized by the French since the seventeenth century and their economies were based on African slavery (abolished in 1848). Both have had *département* status in the French government since 1943, and they share French television and radio, magazines and newspapers, as well as an education system rooted in France. But the two areas also have a well-documented history of African-derived forms of music and dance. Coexisting with them in both rural and urban areas are the formal European dances such as the mazurka, the waltz, and the polka, all of which have undergone considerable creolization. Many of these dances occur in suite form, such as the quadrille, just as they do on many of the Anglophonic islands. A typical folk quadrille from Guadeloupe has two sets of four figures each, with the dance directions provided by a rhythmic chant from the caller. The band is made up of accordion, hand drum, triangle and maracas, and sounds remarkably similar to pre-zydeco, old-time Creole bands of rural black Louisiana. Sudden changes of tempo and melodies within songs are a trait of the quadrille, which is regarded as the most traditional of set dances throughout the region.

Creolization in music and dance complicates questions of origins and dissemination in both Martinique and Guadeloupe. Older written accounts of Martinique suggest that the instrumentation of the orchestras that accompany beguines and mazurkas has been firmly established for years. Typical of this instrumentation are the recordings made in Paris beginning in the late 1920s. L'Orchestre Antillais (1929), for instance, had a New Orleans-like (but trumpet-less) front line of clarinet and trombone, with violin, cello, and drums for harmony and rhythm. (Records made by the Louisiana Five in New Orleans from 1918 to 1920 also employ the same instruments.) In Martinique a similar instrumentation has persisted with small variations until the present, the clarinet and trombone weaving improvised polyphonic lines around a somewhat more complex rhythm than the four-square dance and martial beats of early twentieth-century New Orleans. Nonetheless, the similarities of the musics of the two areas outweigh the differences. In fact, some Creole musicians of New Orleans made records remarkably like those of Martinique in rhythm, melody, and even the vocals in French Creole: Paul Barbarin's "Eh la bas," Kid Ory's "Blanche Touquatoux," and Albert Nicholas' "Mo pas lemme ça," "Salle dame," and "Les oignons" are typical. Some of these songs abruptly shift from biguine rhythms to 4/4 halfway through or on the last chorus, possibly highlighting the artificiality of the conjunction of the two musical forms, but also pointing back to their quadrille-suite origins.

The cultural links between New Orleans and Martinique musical performances do not stop here. New Orleans Creole saxophonist Sidney Bechet and New York pianist Willie "The Lion" Smith assembled a group of American players in 1939 to record what they called "Haitian" biguines such as "Les Sous les Palmiers." The work demonstrated their abilities to play Antillean music with a clarinet and trombone lead. By the same token, musicians of Martinique are often able to play in either biguine or New Orleans jazz styles. Clarinetist Robert Movounzy, for example, is equally competent with mazurkas, biguines, and old New Orleans favorites. Jelly Roll Morton, for that matter, had a repertoire that included waltzes, gallops, and mazurkas ("mazookas," he called them, which would have put him in good company with pianists from the French Caribbean, both in terms of music and pronunciation).

Again, it would be tempting to try to trace influences or sources one way or the other, especially as shipping and trade went on between Paris, St. Pierre in Martinique, and New Orleans until the eruption of the volcano Mt. Pelée destroyed St. Pierre in 1902. But there are complex truths beyond reflexive interactions. Most likely, parallel and independent invention was taking place in both areas during this period, and some forms of what we now call jazz were developed in parallel in and outside the United States.

Musical, stylistic, and performative interaction has continued to be a powerful force in shaping Caribbean and New Orleans music throughout the second half of the twentieth century. By the 1950s the clarinet had lost some favor in the French West Indies (as it had in the U.S.) and the saxophone had largely replaced it, just as the electric bass would come to replace the trombone (which, perhaps, had earlier replaced the deeper-toned drums). French West Indian dance bands in this period often expanded in size and developed into brass, reed, and rhythm sections that played against one another, as did swing bands in the United States. But their earlier jazz-like music did not lead in the same direction as in the States, and instead turned towards other Caribbean popular musics such as those from Cuba and Haiti.

A Festival of Liberation, Protest, Affirmation, and Celebration

Mardi Gras is but one of many festivals that grew not only from the process of creolization, but also from the few ways in which slaves were able to obtain a glimpse of New World freedoms. Slave holidays seem to have existed even under the most repressive imperial regimes. Before Emancipation, in fact, these were commonly the flashpoints of revolt, or if not, of unbridled riots. Afterward, most of them served as archives of past indignities, fueled by a replaying of the moment of emancipation. And again, unsurprisingly, as these festivals serve today as markers of the slave past and the power attending liberation, the most intense moments at their center put into action the greatest number of features identified with Africa. Others of these celebrations, like Pinkster Day in Albany and New York City and the Election Days of black New Englanders, we know only from their descriptions by outsiders who happened to encounter them, or from natives of that region who report them in amused and nostalgic old time stories.

Strangely, some of these celebrations, like the Mummer's and Shooter's Day celebrations in Philadelphia, were taken over by working-class ethnic whites through parish organizations. Following this, there was an attempt to integrate the White Mummer's Day Parade of January 1 with the black Independence Day parade in 1870, as there was a group of Philadelphia West Indians, many of them sellers of pepperpot, that Philadelphia delicacy originally brought from the Caribbean and sold on the streets by West Indian vendors. But again riots occurred, with parts of the black community being burned down.

Not surprisingly, white paraders appeared in blackface and drew on many of the stage conventions of the Ethiopian Serenade style of minstrel entertainment. In a final irony, this style of white imitation of slave holidays was recovered by African Americans throughout the Black Atlantic, leading to festivities in which whites imitated blacks and blacks imitated whites imitating blacks. It is at such moments that the process of creolization becomes self-conscious, as the whites acknowledge the black cultural forms of what they thought of as the "good times" before emancipation.

Complicating matters even further, every one of these carnival-esque moments also has groups, both white and black, who dress and parade as Indians. Just as the New Orleans Indians emerge in the finest self-made costumes as they take to the streets, so you find Indian carnival mas' (masking) groups in the many Caribbean cities that enjoy the Carnival season or elaborate upon Emancipation Day ceremonies.

To be sure, these festivities have grown into important moments in the civic life of a city. In response to the Civil Rights movement, white wearing of blackface is no longer tolerated in Philadelphia (or in New Orleans, though the Zulu parades with blacks in blackface continues the usage with inversionary power). In Philadelphia other parapher-nalia of the blackface show are still found, where the strut, taken from the stage cakewalk, is still danced by anyone venturing into the streets. In the Carolina "low country," white imitation of blacks extends to the use of the local black dialect of Geechee or Gullah, and until recently it was found among elite clubs who performed spir-ituals and told the old stories which they claim are part of their tradition as well.

The story remains consistent from Rio and Bahia and Buenos Aires to Trinidad, from Brooklyn to Little Rock. Men and women brought music, dance, their bodies, and their spirits into a protest of the status quo, an affirmation of their cultural resourcefulness, and a celebration of life and community. The same vision of independence and freedom was seen in the Wilmington, North Carolina, area in Junkanoe celebrations, where masking processions very similar to those in Jamaica, Belize, and elsewhere in the Caribbean were considered dangerous to the existing social order, and by 1910 newspapers in North Carolina were calling for an end to the all-black event.

At its beginnings, the New Orleans Mardi Gras was based on the French Catholic pre-Lenten festivity calendar. It was celebrated in public at first by white men who appeared in blackface and strangely reenacted some of the moves that celebrated the bringing together of slaves from different plantations in the late seventeenth and eighteenth centuries after the crops had been harvested (French "canbrulet," English "cropover." This was a time of serious play, deep play, in which all the resources of the community were called on in an amazing bonfire blast that could easily be interpreted as a riot. Indeed, the authorities saw it as such, but laws and policing have never been able to contain this impulse celebrating Emancipation. Then, after 1834, blacks attempted to integrate the parade, only to be rejected.

For many years thereafter the same conflict was enacted in Trinidad, where blacks attempted to enter Carnival where whites were masked as blacks, and where fights, stabbings, and ultimately the burning of many Port-au-Spain buildings destroyed. In 1891, full-scale riots rampaged through the city. Thus, throughout the region, carnival came to be associated with the possibility of rioting and the need for some form of social control.

The similarities in what came next in the history of celebrations in New Orleans, Trinidad, Philadelphia and the many other places in which carnivalesque occasions arose in the nineteenth century are striking. Groups of African Americans developed parades that commented directly on the civic authority that continued to bar them from participation. Counter-Independence Day parades emerged from the bottomlands or their equivalent. In part they made an ironic statement, especially as they replaced those occasions in the year when riots had occurred in the past. In Philadelphia a black Independence Day parade was also held on August 1 to commemorate the coming of Emancipation to in the British colonies.

In many parts of the South, similar elaborations of the moments of emancipation were celebrated on June 10, "Juneteenth" as it was called in many places in Alabama, Mississippi, Texas, Georgia, and Florida. Some of the festivals bear remarkable similarities to celebrations on plantations in St. Lucia, St. Kitts, the American Virgin Islands. These festivities were dismissed by later commentators (such as V. S. Naipaul) as "kingdoms of the night," as mere fantasied and accommodating reconstructions of an African past and a black New World future. But plantation owners took these celebrations far more seriously and feared their outcomes. (A good account of the development of these celebrations is given fictional form in Paula Marshall's *A Timeless Place, A Chosen People.*)

*   *   *

Perhaps more important than any other similarities between these celebrations is that in each case, whether in Havana, Port of Spain, Rio de Janeiro, Port-au-Prince, or the many others that have come to our notice, the occasion arises because there are actually two parades that continue to affect each other, but delineate the race and class structure of the cities in which they have thrived. The white celebration has maintained the European style of pageantry, often by drawing on contemporary renderings of the Middle Ages, and on the court entertainments in which the rich and mighty asserted their sovereignty.

This was the tone picked up by Mark Twain, when he first visited New Orleans, as recorded in *Life on the Mississippi.*

The largest annual event in New Orleans is something which we arrived too late to sample—the Mardi Gras festivities. I saw the procession of the Mystic Crew of Comus there, twenty-four years ago—with knights and nobles and so on, clothed in silken and golden Paris-made gorgeousnesses, planned and bought for that single night's use; and in their train all manner of giants, dwarfs, monstrosities, and other diverting grotesquerie—a startling and wonderful sort of show, as it filed solemnly and silently down the street in the light of its smoking and flickering torches; but it is said that in these latter days the spectacle is mightily augmented, as to cost, splendor, and variety. There is a chief personage—"Rex"; and if I remember rightly, neither this king nor any of his great following of subordinates is known to any outsider. All these people are gentlemen of position and consequence; and it is a proud thing to belong to the organization; so the mystery in which they hide their personality is merely for romance's sake, and not on account of the police.

Mardi Gras is of course a relic of the French and Spanish occupation. but I judge that the religious feature has been pretty well knocked out of it now. Sir Walter has got the advantage of the gentlemen of the cowl and rosary, and he will stay. His medieval business, supplemented by the monsters and the oddities, and the pleasant creatures from fairy-land, is finer to look at than the poor fantastic inventions and performances of the raveling rabble of the day, and serves quite as well, perhaps, to emphasize the day and admonish men that the grace-line between the worldly season and the holy one is reached.

Well, maybe, but in the neighborhoods of New Orleans in which blacks and *gens de couleur* lived, a different African-related religiosity has been maintained in its own way, not through sectarian command but by drawing on the celebratory motive as a way of marking death and continuing life in the area under parade. New Orleans jazz, as we know from the ubiquitous legend of its birth, emerged in part from the bands' march for a funeral of a noteworthy within the community. The first- and the second-lines, through which many African American mutual aid and enjoyment societies display their esteem for one of their members, provide the primary style of playing Mardi Gras in that part of town.

On the other side of town, often in the neighborhoods that are presumed, because of poverty, not to have any culture at all, they have developed their own system of celebration around the same occasion. Organized by neighborhoods and clubs and beneficial associations that extend beyond even those parts of town, these festivities seem to have emerged from slaves' holidays held before Emancipation. And, not incidentally, in these a great many of the most African-derived features of performance have been maintained and embroidered upon.

Where such celebrations have become tourist events, the two ways of parading comment upon each other in a great many ways. Some of the most important characteristics of the African American parade are the formal elements, features that unite these parades within and without Mardi Gras celebrations. The first and most obvious is the stance used by some of those in front of the parade. The left hand is placed on the hip and the right hand is extended upward, forming half of what is called "akimbo." This stance is associated with other postural elements, such as the swaying of the hips, or a one-legged position and a back-bending (sometimes all the way to the ground behind) posture.

Folklorist Harold Courlander encountered this stance in Haiti in the 1930s, where it was called the "Kongo pose" in recognition of its sources: in the Kongo such as posture is known as the *diguimbu* stance, a woman's iconographic posture, where it is understood that the left hand presses down evil while the right hand vibrates positively for the future. It is a stance of authority, used to send warriors to their success, in lawsuits to dissolve marriages, and the like. In Haiti today it is said that the left hand holds down evil while the right hand signifies that Christ has risen. In the United States today this stance is also encountered among storytellers who use the gesture to make certain authoritative points.

Drum majors and majorettes use this stance, and when we note what they have in their right hands we move even further into the realm of African American cultural history, for so much of the vocabulary of celebrating at sporting events and parades has entered into

American vernacular life from African power displays. In Colombia and Ecuador a calabash (a form of bottle gourd) is held up during processions. Such a calabash was also in the hands of celebrants in Congo Square in New Orleans in 1825, and can be seen in Brazil's carnival today. Colonel Thomas Higginson, who led a group of African American soldiers during the American Civil War, tells us in *Army Life in a Black Regiment* (1870) that the black soldiers he commanded in the Civil War were led on marches by a washerwoman with a long-handled silver drinking cup which she swung over her head.

The baton would seem to be the most European element of parading and marching, but Colonel Higginson also noted that in the 1860s he saw a cakewalker with a pot on his head twirling a baton and bending backward, suggesting that the baton was quite early on radically transformed from the simple swagger stick of the European officer (or even the king's scepter, for that matter). And indeed in Haiti during Holy Week, the RaRa bands are led by figures called Major Joncs, who twirl and throw silver batons made out of light metal, dipping to the ground, spinning face to face, battling with each other. The combative use of batons is echoed in the sticks carried by the Mardi Gras Indians of New Orleans, and in stick-fighting found in Trinidad and elsewhere in the West Indies.

Similar displays of objects held in this manner at the head of the parade are found throughout the Black Atlantic. Brooms are held and spun around in the parades of Montevideo's processions, much as they are in the Kongo. In Trinidad's carnival they are carried and tossed by figures called Moko Jumbis. In many islands of the West Indies walking sticks are also twirled and tossed, much as they were by African American dancers in the nineteenth-century formal dance called the cakewalk.

The early black stage performers Bert Williams and George Walker included in their routine in the 1890s a character who was a drum major and did a baton twirling routine, and white minstrel T. D. "Daddy" Rice also imitated such African American figures in the nineteenth century, long before white bands adopted twirling drum majors. In other cases, white minstrel men blacked up and dressed as women to twirl batons.

Umbrellas, both furled and unfurled, are seen in the Mardi Gras and jazz funeral marches of New Orleans, in Brazil, in the brushback dance of Trinidad, and again among the cakewalk dancers in the United States in the nineteenth and early twentieth centuries. Ribbons are attached to the top of the open umbrellas, and feathered birds are used as finials, much as among the Asante people of Southern Ghana and elsewhere in Africa. The umbrella's use in New Orleans parades is symbolic, rhythmic, and practical in serving as parasols against the blistering sun. These highly decorated umbrellas are not used in the rain, however (though the folks who show up carrying umbrellas and wearing Burberry raincoats to second-line the Preservation Hall Band's concerts at Wolf Trap in Virginia seem to have not gotten the point).

The spinning, twirling, and tossing of objects in parades is not a European convention. It was introduced to European and Euro-Americans by Africans and peoples of African descent. In the late 1700s the African drum corps then in fashion in European military bands used batons in an animated fashion, far from the proper one-two of white commanders. Nor was the juggling limited to batons: Leigh Hunt, a friend of Lord Byron's, describing one marching event on Pall Mall in London, remarked that one of the African drummers "threw his cymbals into the sun," and was amazed that he caught them before they came down on the heads of the other marchers.

Nor are drum majorettes part of European tradition. There was no place for women in marching bands in Europe for many years, and even now it is the exception rather than the rule. No American bands had majorettes before the 1920s, either, and some older Southerners recall when only African American women marched with bands. The Major Joncs in Haitian RaRa are dressed as women, as are some of the marchers in St. Vincent, in nineteenth-century South Carolinian festivals, and in the Western Girls Band of New Orleans Mardi Gras.

The acceptance of women into marching bands may have occurred first in the United States, but it was not without resistance. Commenting on the paramilitary visage of majorettes, Marshall McLuhan as late as the 1950s could ask: "Who dreamed up that goose stepping combination of military mechanism and bootjack eroticism? That ludicrous hodgepodge of uncontrollable desires and imbecilic motions." And later, posters for the infamous film *Myra Breckenridge* would show Raquel Welsh (a transvestite in the movie) dressed and posed as a majorette. Handbooks on baton twirling distort this complex history as might be expected, but in interesting ways. First, they root the origins of majorettes in southern girls' schools in the late 1800s. Then, in Constance Atwater's *On Baton Twirling: The Fundamentals of an Art and Skill,* she notes of the majorette's stance: "You want to achieve a saucy little body movement so that you don't feel like a highstepping zombie." As Robert Farris Thompson observed, she unwittingly calls up the name of both god and a corpse in the Kongo. The faces and genders may have changed, but from urging on warriors to urging athletes there is nonetheless a kind of continuity. In New Orleans, like the rest of the South, the teenaged black female baton twirler in skin-tight spangled suits with a body stocking covering bare arms and legs is the focus of rapt attention by the crowds. Boys in the age bracket and older men often cheer and leer within and across lines of race and class. For girls—along with synchronized dancers and the less mobile members of the band's flag corps— competition to be part of these marching displays begins in junior high school. Mothers and female chaperones—wary of the sensual aspects of the display—are often quick to point out to the bystander, "We are teaching them to use what they have to be . . . ladies."

* * *

Most significantly, in every case of metropolitan Carnivals in the Greater Caribbean, the racial divide remains absolute in certain dimensions, thus intensifying the power of local knowledge. There are actually two major Carnivals taking place simultaneously. In New Orleans one of them is said to have begun with the Cowbellions and other such groups, and then mutated into the various elite Krewes, who now draw on the devices of European royal pageantry or medieval tournaments. This group of celebrations is held almost exclusively indoors, in private, and are celebrated without the outside world knowing much more than what they learn when the Krewes actually parade. The other carnival, according to legend, is said to have emerged from the celebrations in Congo Square and to represent the continuing presence of Africa in the Mardi Gras imagination. Here one continues to find certain secret practices and arcane knowledge being drawn on to give torque to the festival moment.

The contribution of black dancers to New Orleans history centered on old Congo Square, located between what is now the New Orleans Municipal Auditorium and Rampart Street. There, in the early nineteenth century, African dancing was visible to the public. Blacks danced in circles, miniature citadels of spirit and certainty. Kongo competed with other African peoples in the formation of local culture. Prominent among these were the Mande, Yoruba, and Fon. But the Bakongo were singularly influential in dance. Numerous dances named "Congo" were recorded in nineteenth-century Louisiana, along with the Kongo-derived bamboula. Whole systems of motion and gesture crossed the Atlantic and took root in the city and parishes. An immediate example is nzuba, a thigh-slapping dance from kingdom of Kongo. The name derives from the Ki-Kongo verb "to slap": zuba. With a lightly creolized title—"juba" or "patting juba"—it spread up the river and diffused far and wide. Among the Black Hawk spiritualist churches of African American New Orleans, it is one of the steps that come back from the past when people dance in the spirit.

This technique of using the body as an instrument is probably as important as any rhythmic technique in transporting African, and especially Kongo, metric sensibilities to New World settings. Drums do not lend themselves to surviving the transatlantic journey, but the human body endures. Its use in patting juba was only one way in which the body and hands were used to externalize the rhythmic pulse, the timeline of African music. And with this patting or clapping was carried a deep sense of connectedness to each other, to the past. It would become an especially useful technique of communication when patting juba was used to warn each other of the presence of the night riders, later the Ku Klux Klan, which folklorist and historian Gladys-Marie Fry considered in her study of post-bellum black/white relations in the South.

In the form of patting juba, the dance became something of a the-atrical craze in the middle of the nineteenth century when it was used by a dancer who called himself Juba, described by the visitor Charles Dickens while on a lecture tour. In handclapping routines, juba seems to have survived in a form associated with shoeshine patter well into the mid-twentieth century, where it organized itself around the idea of the jawbone—"Jawbone walk and jawbone talk / jawbone eat with a knife and fork"—and hambone—"Hambone, hambone, have you heard, / Papa gonna buy you a marking bird." Roger Abrahams heard both children and young men on the corner in South Philadel-phia performing this routine for twenty minutes at a time, with virtu-oso patters, using cupped hands clapped on one or another body part, and set up by each performer apart from and in contrast to oth-ers using different sounds on other parts of the body. This was in the late 1950s about the time that the rhythm 'n' blues artist Bo Diddley began to musicalize the rhythm in his singing stage routines, provid-ing one of the strongest links to contemporary practices of hip-hop or rap. All the while, young black girls had kept the practice alive, in the form of their handclapping games.

African Americans, like the Bakongo with nzuba, play with the entire body. From a notice of dancing in Georgia dated 1851: "Some one calls for a fiddle—but if one is not to be found, someone 'pats juber.' This is done by placing one foot a little in advance of the other, raising the ball of the foot from the ground, and striking it in regular time, while, in connection, the hands are struck slightly together, and then upon the thighs." This performance was observed later by Lafcadio Hearn in Cincinnati, where he heard black roust-abouts on the levees singing, "frequently accompanied with that wonderfully rapid slapping of thighs and hips know as patting juba." Slapping thighs was composing time-lines, percussion to dance by.

Followers of the Kongo classical religion believe that zuba is medicine. Zuba builds confidence through rough forms of massage (zyola); slapping your body, it is argued, deepens aliveness. Thigh-slapping dance also emerged among Kongo-influenced dancers in Lima, Peru, and among Angola-influenced martial artists in Bahia, Brazil, where patting juba is called bate cox. In the United States today it is called hambone—because you are hitting your thigh, your hambone.

Spinning solo in place—pirouetting—is frequent in Kongo, where they call it bangúmuka, "turning," or nzyeta, "turning around." Conceptually a turn "ties a knot" (kango kolo) in the action, providing punctuation and aesthetic interest. Such a move, or motion, as they call it in the ring game found in black enclaves in the United States and throughout the ex-British West Indies, calls on dancers in the center of a ring-play to show out, show their stuff, shake their body, whatever. Robert Farris Thompson has called attention to this element, terming it, suggestively, "apart playing." In fact, it is the central and organizing figure in all the ring-plays found through the Greater Caribbean. As such, it stands at the center of the lessons in play and in life that Georgia Sea Island leader Bessie Jones taught the whole of her adult life.

This aesthetic depends not only on playing apart, but on voices and bodies interacting in such a way that they overlap and interlock in movement and voice. The much discussed call-and-response way of organizing singing at work as at play comes to the fore in African-styled performance throughout the hemisphere. Here the drama, even the religious impact of the aesthetic is underscored as the dancers set their faces in a cool manner, while they encourage the body to do the heating up. The contrast between heat and cool informs much of African based religious and secular dance throughout the Western Hemisphere, a contrast seen more in the dynamic interaction of the two attitudes rather than in competition with each other.

Such an oppositional arrangement achieves sacred form in the ring-shout, which historian Sterling Stuckey sees as the central motif in New World African-derived worship. The ring-shout can still be observed in some congregations in the United States, such as the worship bands described by Jonathan David on the Eastern and Western Shores of Maryland, or the well documented Watch Night ceremonies of groups like the McIntosh County Shouters from the George Sea Islands. Here, as in the Congolese rituals, the ring is divided in four, making what Robert Farris Thompson has called a cosmogram, a map of the spiritual universe. The ways this arrangement is established among the Kongo are not very different from the ways it is discussed by the exegetes of the word in Maryland, David finds. Congolese patterns of movement and worship, drumming and dancing provide the lingua franca for all the Transatlantic Black World—a way of organizing and calling down the spirit. In all formulations, sacred movement serves as a ghost of the profane and vice versa. The two are not so easily separated in this area of the world, since they are so firmly connected when the spirit descends on the congregation, or in the procession electing the Negro King on Pinkster Day in nineteenth-century New England, or, for that matter, in the second-line at black Mardi Gras.

A dynamic opposition emerges in two styles of eloquence as well, two attitudes toward communication: one is hot, the other not. The coolest speak in elevated codes, kingly talk, courtly talk, full of declamatory flourish. Many of the festivities in the Greater Caribbean focus on activities in which performers are presented as speakers of great distinction, capable of making pronouncements in this most elevated style of regal cool. Roger Abrahams, who has been tracking such figures since late in the 1950s, calls them "Men-of-Words," in that they express their power through their ability to improvise in words—admitting when confronted that the term is sexist, and that there are very many women who command these varieties of self-presentation. Some show their knowledge through high oratory and grandiloquence. Others, more nimble with their tongues and more sly and rapid in their delivery, demonstrate their combative abilities through being aggressive, assertive, given to expression in the most openly creole displays using language of the streets. It is called *picong* in Trinidad, rapping, capping, or signifying in the United States. To put the style in terms used today, it is a display of attitude, talking trash, getting in each other's face, and showboating. Such talk inspires admiration for its quickness, its ability to heat up speech. Rather than stately, it is brazen, quick, combative. It is breathtaking, though not always admired except in the highly contestive situations that arise during Carnival when two groups, representing the pride of a neighborhood, encounter each other on the street and engage in a verbal battle.

In the last decade, a pair of dazzling books by Australian historians Shane White and Graham White read the whole story of black life in America in terms suggesting the ubiquity of the Kongo way of organizing the world and embellishing it with meaning and feeling. Following up on the exhaustive scholarship of Dena Epstein that surveyed the entire repertoire of African American expressive culture, the Whites find riches aplenty in the periodical literature, diaries, and eyewitness accounts of how this aesthetic undergirds clothing, hair style, cuisine, or just stepping out or hanging out.

Mardi Gras serves as the apotheosis of this style of elaborate and deliberate marching out in this yearly moment of liberation. It is difficult to conceive of the event without the presence of Indian bands. When their group marches out during Mardi Gras, they are fearlessly feathered and gloriously garbed. They wear expressions of red and black unity. Battles of dress keep the art moving. The Indians come out not just to parade but to conquer, much as do the leaders of Speech Mas' on Tobago, brave warriors typical of Carnival contestants.

The *boismen* of Trinibago, the *capoeira* dancer-combatants of Rio, and the Guardians of the Flame Mardi Gras Indians in New Orleans all march to the same agonistic pulses. Calypso was born in such an environment, but then so was Samba, emerging from the *sambista* societies engaged in combat each year at Brazilian Carnaval. Again, as Donald Harrison put it: "Put the confrontation on. If you don't meet nobody, you're just walking down the street." He need not have added, if you do meet others, let the battle rage.

Elaborate costumes are the prerogative of the big chiefs, broadcasting their rank and authority. Surprise, bedazzlement is a part of that power. Again Harrison: "Next year I'll come out in a wild shade of blue—and smoke all those suckers." Bo Dollis, Big Chief of the Wild Magnolias, astonished New Orleans in 1983 with a costume that virtually transformed him into a huge feathered totem pole. Distinct to the tradition are "patches," defined by photographer Michael Smith in *Spirit World*, his fine book on Mardi Gras dazzle, "as a tableau made out of beads, sequins, and other materials sewn into canvas," and sewn, in the main, by the chief himself. They are cognate with beaded and sequined panels worn by maskers in Trinidad, which themselves are amazingly close to the beaded and appliquéd panels of Egungun costumes in Yorubaland in Nigeria. Some New Orleans "Indians" are seamen and keep in touch with visual action elsewhere in the Caribbean, as they have done for all of their history. The resemblances are far from coincidental. Chiefs in New Orleans and Trinidad read voraciously, seeking ideas from handbooks and encyclopedias as well as dreams and observations of others. Authenticity of costumes is not always absolute, but it is always highly valued. And if the culture being borrowed from visually also has a hierarchy reflected in its indigenous costumes, that is all the better to borrow from.

African New Orleans does not rest on its laurels. New Orleans and the parishes, especially around Lafayette, pepper sensibilities with creative change. Consider the musical innovation in black Creole settings around Lafayette, St. Martin, St. Landry, and other parishes of southwest Louisiana: from *la-la* (old Creole dance music) to *juré* (testifying chants with body percussion and vocal fricatives that Alan Lomax described as "the most African sound I found in America") to zydeco, a sound that has taken its place in the World Music movement.

Isaac Holmes, a visitor to Louisiana in 1821, saw blacks moving to the beat of a drum on their own making. "The general movement is what they call the Congo dance." Along the Ouachita River in northern Louisiana, before 1833, Theodore Pavie witnessed a Central African ritual among blacks celebrating the capture of a wild cat. In Kongo, just to touch the skin of a wild cat is associated with celebration, for the feline is famous as a mediator between worlds, roaming both forest and village. Kongo noblemen linked themselves with that boundary-crossing power by wearing small wild cat aprons. Such animal figures who wander back and forth between the bush and the village populate the nine-night (wake) stories found from the Saramakka of Surinam to the Cockpit Maroons of Jamaica, and are still found in Anansi stories told at wakes in many of the Windward and Leeward Islands—not only Brer Rabbit lives on, sometimes as *lapin*, but also Anansi, the spider, and as well as the clever slave, John going up against Ol' Marster.

In the early nineteenth century black women and men momentarily regained their nationality when they danced in Congo Square and out in the parishes, much as did the descendents of those from West Indian island Carriacou, who annually reaffirm their ties to each other and to Africa through the Big Drum Nation Dances. This back-referencing is even more profound in the dance-songs and rituals of Maroon communities, carved from the bush by runaway slaves in Guyana, Jamaica, and Surinam and the Garifuna of Belize, studied so brilliantly by Richard and Sally Price and their student and colleague Ken Bilby.

The critical stylistic and ethical continuity from the Kongo and other parts of Sub-Saharan African involves the holy act of dancing called shouting, not because of the noise it makes, but from the holy jumping or *saut* of Muslim Africa. The shout emerges from within the circles in Old Time Religion black churches in the United States. To enter a circle is to enter deep blackness, to receive secret strength in contact with ecstasy. The circle is round like the sun's timeless path, like the time-defying spiral of the seashells placed on black graves in the McDonoughville cemetery of Gretna, Louisiana. It is a medicine of continuity and protection. For the Bakongo, dancing is life itself ("makanu I zingu kiau kibeni"), and that impulse toward permanence, cycling through space with percussion, was not cultivated in vain.

The drums of Congo Square did not disappear at the closing of that tradition in the mid-nineteenth century. It keeps reappearing, phoenix like, in, say, the fields at the edge of Lake Ponchartrain, north of New Orleans, as reported in 1831, at a place the blacks call "the camp." Here Africans and their friends came together in distinct ethnic groups gathering under flags of their nations. On May 1, 1808, one Christian Schultz saw twenty different dancing groups in Congo Square, each ensemble performing its own national dance. The instruments of one of the nations included long narrow drums two to eight feet in length; these were the *gdungu*, the long drums of North Kongo, where they were played to stimulate ecstasy. This experience was replicated wherever groups, often called tambo-bambo throughout the Caribbean, took assorted lengths of cut bamboo that they hollowed out and hammered on the ground, and raised and lowered them rhythmically, creating an effect not unlike African Bantu hocketing—staggered, overlapping rhythmic melodies, with different notes assigned to each player.

The lead dancers in the Kongolese *ngungu* gyrated to drumming in Congo Square wearing tails of the smaller wild animals. They were flaunting the spiritual side of the culture. In Kongo, tailed dress represents sacred medicine, the much discussed *nkisi*, now adopted by some New Age religious practitioners. Their spiritual power is undisputable, even to the most skeptical audiences.

Nor do such onlookers doubt the power embodied in "getting down"—mixing strong leans with deep knee bends. These went straight into the ring-shouts of the churches and the street corner break dances and the march of the drum majorettes at predominantly black colleges in the United States, as dance historian Jaqui Malone has shown in her book, *Steppin' on the Blues*. Throughout the Black Atlantic, getting down is getting down, and breaking out is just what it says, making a break or a cut for the sake of dramatic power, or for the strong cutting and break out runners in American football. All these terms and the movements they designate are at the center of what Robert Farris Thompson calls the "aesthetic of the cool."

Given the clear impact of Kongo on the square bearing its name, it is likely that the two women dancers noted by architect Benjamin Latrobe in his journal, with white kerchiefs before their bodies, held in one or both hands, were clearing the way to glory, purifying the space, spiritually protecting all followers. That is, they were doing more than merely decorating the dance and adding to their sexual allure, as we find in European couple dancing, but were sweeping away personal and social problems alike, protecting themselves and their kin with a gesture outsiders saw only as a flourish.

Latrobe visited another dancing group in the Place Congo. Here women shuffled round the musicians, the time-line produced by a slit gong struck with a stick. There was a square drum resembling a stool with a leather seat, and a calabash drum beaten by a woman with two short sticks. The calabash drum had a round hole studded with a circle of brass nails, the traditional strong way of protecting the drummer from the negative. All these instruments—the frame drum, the slit gong, and the calabash drum—are known in Kongo.

According to Felipe García Villamil, a leading priest of the Kongo religion in Cuba, an initiate's possession is genuine when only the whites of the eyes show. Bembe sculpture captures this state by showing "eyes that roll up." Michael P. Smith in *Spirit World* has an image of persons in New Orleans "falling out." Just as the white eyes relate spiritual people to Bembe sculpture, so the famous New Orleans faith healer Mother Catherine Seals, who lived in the now lamented lower Ninth Ward, before she died in 1930 made herself a spectacular robe beaded with the image of Jesus armed with a similar optic. Jesus guards her with the spiritual light of his eyes. They blaze with whiteness, like the white porcelain eyes found in Bembe figures. The physical and spiritual reminders are all in place, for those who would recover them.

The percussion of Congo Square continued and surfaced in the drums of Baby Dodds, in the scraped washboards of early black jug bands, which have parallels in the *frottoirs* (rub-boards) of Creole zydeco music. The washboards become vests in zydeco bands, carrying the rhythm complexities along with an accordion, a trap set, and other instruments. The frottoir is worn bib-style and made into a rhythm instrument when scraped by a metal object like a spoon or a thimble or a church-key bottle opener. When the brothers Clifton and Cleveland Chenier used the frottoir in the 1950s, they took black percussion one degree higher to a broader public beyond Creole Louisiana. They were not just expressing the beat, they were wearing it.

Congo Square was reborn in the rise of the spasm band, which improvised instruments as well as music. The first documented spasm band—they had existed earlier, below the radar, as New Orleans educator Al Kennedy reminds us—played the streets of New Orleans around 1896. The tradition flowed on, to 1948, when the authors of

Mardi Gras Day spotted such percussionists on a Vieux Carré street: "The spasm band goes down Royal Street and lingers near a crowd that looks happy. The leader gives the beat, and the washboard rhythms, from tin cans, wire and homemade percussion instruments, begin."

Spasm bands link the drum choirs of Congo Square to the integrated jazz battery. Amateur drummers ruled Royal Street in the 2004 Mardi Gras. Spaced along the sidewalk, one-man spasm bands played upside-down dry-wall-compound plastic buckets with sticks. Peter "J. J." Chatwick, a local African American, manned his post in front of the Monteleone Hotel. Farther east, Chris Harris, a young white man from Tampa, Florida, played the same improvised drum kit in much the same style. Between them worked "Tony Pots-and-Pans," a man of color whose stage name betrayed a taste for bright metal instruments: as well as his buckets he played metal grates and a square piece of chrome, for flash and resonance.

All three drummers hit the tops of their pails to make a high note and lifted a pail with their right foot, then dropped it down while hitting it. "That gives us our bass," Chris Harris explained. The idea of modifying the tones of a drum with the foot is Central African. It came to New Orleans, and to Guadeloupe and other places in the Caribbean, with Bakongo drum masters. The concept inspired the invention of the bass drum with foot pedal in jazz. (The different tones of the heel and toe of tap shoes, derived indirectly, are a distant echo of the same foot-tone configuration.)

Throughout the Greater Caribbean, African American musicians found work as musicians and dancemasters, demonstrating their versatility even under slavery. During the same period when musicians and dance leaders were achieving a place in New Orleans, on Martinique and Guadeloupe the adaptation of European musical instruments to African-based time-lines was creating a music not unlike jazz, an independent invention but so like what occurred at the birth of ragtime that the parallels are worth much further study, as are the developments that occurred in Havana with the birth of the son style, rediscovered by American audiences in Ry Cooder's film and recording of the Buena Vista Social Club.

*   *   *

In all these places the percussion traditions of the slaves and newly liberated freedmen opened vistas for the development of popular forms of music and dance that have remained vital, even as one after another is rediscovered. The drums and slit-gongs of Congo Square were so powerfully voiced that they easily recrystallized around Western instruments. The transfer took place by the 1830s and '40s, as the last African drum makers began to die out. Later, in 1860 or 1881, Lafcadio Hearn witnessed two black men beating found object drums while old persons danced with tin rattles on their ankles in a wood yard on Dumaine Street in the Quarter. One drum was a dry-goods box, the other was a pork barrel. They beat them with sticks and with bones. Read this two ways—as a fugitive expression of Congo Square music and simultaneously a rising manifestation of improvised percussion, spasm-band style.

This kind of ankle rattle is still found throughout both the New World and much of the Old, associated with the Moorish or Morris or Moresco dance, often in combination with other attached metal objects making sounds in different timbres and textures, such as rattling devices. Sweet Emma Barrett, the "Bell Gal," was a New Orleans pianist best known for the bells she attached to her garters. Jingle Bells indeed, as well as the tambourines, the shak-shak, and other rhythm-enriching hand-held objects held above now one ear, now the other. The tambourines of the nineteenth century continue as twenty-first-century tambourines by the same name among the black spiritual churches of New Orleans and many other places. They also resurface in tambourines and iron gongs among the famed Indian maskers of Mardi Gras, among other neighborhood music makers in the black Mardi Gras.

Indeed, there are few gestures to be found at the heart of Mardi Gras or the second-lines and jazz funerals on that side of town that do not yield such meanings and understandings, all projected through the aesthetic of the cool, and put into action by the amazing array of benevolent and friendly societies in those parts.

Carnival Knowledge: Mardi Gras in and Beyond New Orleans

Mardi Gras is historically associated with French and Spanish populations along the Gulf Coast. However, many groups such as Anglo-American and Jewish cultural elites in Uptown New Orleans, Gays in the French Quarter, and African American middle-class men and women in Mobile now join in the traditional festive occasion. Mardi Gras falls on the Tuesday in February or March prior to Ash Wednesday and, hence, forty days before Easter. The Mediterranean-Latin roots of Mardi Gras are in the pre-Roman rites of spring and later Roman festival or ritual occasions such as Baccanalia, Lupercalia, and Saturnalia. Over time, were incorporated into the Catholic liturgical calendar as a means of controlling occasions of sensory excess and boundary breaking—many of which offer anticlerical critiques through satire and lampooning.

Just as Roman Catholicism absorbed earlier pre-Roman Carnival elements, so too the worldwide variations on Carnival now express regional cultural and social diversity, creolization at its richest and finest. Gulf Coast Carnival, like Carnival in related societies of the Caribbean and Latin America, is a series of local creolizations of French/Spanish, Native American, and African/Afro-Caribbean cultural encounters played out in various performance styles and structures. That the earliest European settlers of the Gulf Coast celebrated Mardi Gras is suggested by the explorer D'Iberville, who named a portion of land below Lake Ponchartrain and east of the Mississippi River "Mardi Gras Bayou." Informal parades and festive masquerades are reported to have occurred in major centers like Mobile and New

Orleans throughout the early nineteenth century, and by midcentury (1857, to be exact, in New Orleans) officially sanctioned parades began.

The Gulf Coast Carnival season officially begins on January 6—the Twelfth Day of Christmas, Epiphany, Feast of Kings. On this date in New Orleans "King Cakes"—with a plastic miniature baby inside each and adorned in Mardi Gras colors of gold, purple, and green— are consumed in celebration. The season may be as short as three and a half weeks or as long as two months, depending on the date of Easter. The culmination of Carnival is Mardi Gras day or Shrove Tuesday in English usage (referring to being "shriven of one's sins"). The festive eating, dancing, drinking, and public sexuality associated with Mardi Gras are followed by the relative austerity and penitence of the Lenten period.

The early official parades in New Orleans and Mobile were founded by the Anglo and Creole (French/Spanish) elites of both cities. In New Orleans, such krewes as Comus, Momus, Proteus, and Rex continue from the nineteenth century into the present. In the 1990s, when the city passed ordinances requiring open admission and the potential for including African Americans, several of the old-line elite groups ceased their public parades. Although many blacks in the city had no special desire to ride in these krewes, some of the old-line groups agreed in principle, if not practice, to open their membership. Others have since ceased parading and only hold private balls. The still essentially segregated elite krewes are seen by street audiences of black and white, rich and poor, that are as fully integrated as New Orleans itself.

These crowds can have huge agency in responding to elite float motifs and heroes. For example, Nick Spitzer reports that a few years ago, when the Confederate flag controversy was rising again (never as big an issue in New Orleans as in Mississippi and Georgia), about a dozen black men in their twenties showed up at the Krewe d'Etat's nighttime parade in the heart of its Uptown St. Charles street turf wearing floppy Cat in the Hat headgear emblazoned with the "Stars and Bars" of the Confederacy. Their posture was, "You wanna do Old School control with that flag? It's also ours to play with at Mardi Gras!"

Spitzer describes another encounter in the Tremé neighborhood on the downtown home turf of Afro-Creole folks, where a group of elderly men dressed as hillbillies in overalls with corncob pipes, mountaineer hats, jugs of moonshine, and, in a city with a high murder rate, old double barrel shotguns. They were headed for the French Quarter.

More recently, the pro-war activist and right-wing country singer Toby Keith was made an honorary king of one Uptown parade, only to have his entourage splattered by paint balls fired from the crowd. Keith had been glowering at the assembled masses, with his seconds threatening those in the crowd who thought he was a poor choice for a night of mirth. "Deep play all the way," remarked Spitzer.

These old-line krewes pride themselves on using smaller antique-style floats depicting mythological scenes crafted in papier-mâché. Their relative wealth and power gives them access to teams of artists and designers that maintain a rarified vision of the parades' "heritage." The floats were originally drawn by mules, mostly replaced by tractors in the 1950s. The artwork found on newer floats is made of plastic and fiberglass, and float-making has become more and more tied to world tourism sites, providing annual work for other mobile celebrations worldwide and clients like Disney. Tourists may visit Mardi Gras World—a combination showroom, construction site, and warehouse of Mardi Gras floats and figures—operated as a family business by Blaine Kern on New Orleans' West Bank. Globalization has operated in a reverse way as well, as Kern has long recruited Italian carnival float artists and buildings to his New Orleans mega-shop.

As many as sixty different krewes parade in the roughly two-week period prior to and including Mardi Gras day. Some, such as Arabi and Argus, are quite recent and represent suburban neighborhoods.

All parades throw doubloons (introduced in the early 1960s) and other plastic trinkets to the crowds that line such primary parade routes as St. Charles Avenue and Canal Street. The varied krewes both reflect and invert the social structure of New Orleans on a day when the upper classes play at being kings, fools, and mythological beings. Suburban middle classes may assert their right to be royalty for a day. Elite old-line krewes maintain an aura of secrecy about the selection of their royalty and invitations to their balls and affiliated social events. Newer krewes such as Bacchus and Endymion, on the other hand, charge admission to their open gatherings in the Superdome and elsewhere at the end of parades.

In contrast to the old and new wealthy, exclusive and less so white elite krewes are the walking societies: originally white working-class groups of men who parade loosely in costume along main routes and also back streets with visits to neighborhood bars. Among these are clarinetist Pete Fountain's wryly named "Half Fast" walking club and the Jefferson City Buzzards, who operate from a small clubhouse and neighborhood barroom on the River side of Uptown.

Until about two decades ago, the Buzzards often went in blackface. They have since removed that approach to masking in response to criticism and political evolution with a younger generation. The Buzzards generally attempt to look regal in a sort of overdressed, foolhardy way, wearing capes and bearing imitation flowers that they dispense in exchange for kisses along the route. While the Buzzards focus on young white women, the Mardi Gras day crowd is heavily mixed, and their kissing crosses the lines of color, class, and age—to the delight, dismay, or disgust of the recipients. In the weeks prior to their increasingly drunken Carnival day walk from back streets out onto the prime time real estate of St. Charles Avenue—usually after Zulu but before the Rex parade—the Buzzards are also noted for an Uptown march in drag. Like many heterosexual imitations of women in the Mardi Gras season, the emphasis is on the grotesque, as the often unshaven Buzzards wear ill-fitting wigs and short skirts over hairy legs, sporting huge breasts with large, defined nipples. They may act out tantrums and raucous speeches, hitting one another with their small pocketbooks and generally lampooning women. In contrast, the downtown French Quarter to Bywater Gay male crossdressers of Mardi Gras often emphasize an elegant and, they hope, sexually attractive image of femininity enhanced by plantation belle dress or the image of glamorous Vieux Carré courtesans

A further distinction can be made between the kind of activities fostered by the Uptown elite white krewes like Momus and Rex and the African American and Creole neighborhood masking, singing, dancing individuals and societies. The former is a dyed in the wool American club activity. Moreover, the Uptown elite krewes of this once Latin festive occasion are dominated by Protestants who have transformed Carnival from its French Spanish colonial roots in the city to a kind of waspy play party of noblesse oblige, where they dutifully inscribe their mission on Rex doubloons as Pro Bono Publico ("For the Public Good"). Social historian Lawrence Powell describes the elite Uptown Carnival as "Protestant gentlemen at the apex of a Catholic festival spending most of the year organizing balls and cotillions for their wives and daughters. The deeply symbolic rituals are different too. No rites of reversal here. . . . New Orleans' version is an occasion for exemplifying the status regime, not inverting it."

The creolized and un-American activities surrounding the "other" Mardi Gras in black American Central City and farther downtown in the Afro-Creole wards present a different story, one connected with the rest of the Greater Caribbean and Black Atlantic. As Peter Clark, the historian of volunteer associations on both sides of the Atlantic, put it, "the growth of clubs and societies should be seen as part of the wider development of public sociability"—a natural outgrowth of the new value placed on gregariousness, good manners, and male bonding on the basis of the principles of good fellowship, "the expression of a dynamic, increasingly urban society in which the traditional structures of corporate and communal life were either absent or inappropriate for the full range of contemporary conditions and aspirations." Others have put forward that clubs were a development on the virtues of a distinctive bourgeois identity, and inevitably in the academic climate of the last few decades, they are regarded as part and parcel of the development of the "public sphere."

The story of the formation of the Cowbellion de Rakin Society, which began in Mobile but moved to New Orleans in the 1830s, is totally in line with the thousands of other groups of male carousers that developed just before and after the American Revolution. In this, Americans were following the pattern of the British civilizing enterprise in conceiving of these groups as representing the best way of exercising civility. Members of such organizations actually seem to have seen themselves as on the cutting edge of civic development, albeit on the informal side.

In the large commercial cities of the East Coast such as Boston, Philadelphia, Annapolis, and Charleston, the activities of the voluntary associations arose from common interest and included many educational and ethnic support groups. But even those that met for noble purpose did so in taverns—often the best gathering place in town—as they gravitated toward the dining out and drinking activities so beloved by men on the move financially. and looking for ways to get out of the house once a week or month. These groups, many still in existence, often took on jocular exotic names. Historian Stephen Bullock, reporting on the range of these organizations, opined, "The conviviality that was a secondary purpose of nearly all charitable groups became the primary purpose of many others." One Bostonian visiting Charleston in 1773 attended meetings of the Candlestick Club, the Smoking Club, the Segoon-Pop Club, and the Beef-Steak Club.

This was a transatlantic club movement, with local groups taking on antic names dreamed up by one wag club member or another. They differ, of course, from the Freemasons, who claimed ancient lineage and origins in a medieval craft guild. On the other hand, like the Masons, they often had an elaborate ritual of initiation, a hierarchy, and songs that served as club anthems, whether serious or otherwise.

Which is not to say that such organizations were only found in cities. Perhaps of a more occasional sort, most frontier outposts boasted of building various lodges soon after their formation. If the Grange had not yet come into preferment by farmers, there were certainly an enormous number of Masonic lodges in country villages, towns, and cities.

An important feature of their life as groups was to enter the public parades of the community, and so they do to this day. Wearing their badge of office, they assemble in their official dress—or is it costume—holding the badge of office if as individuals they have ascended to power. Each war seems to have generated its own venerable organization, like the American Legion, Veterans of Foreign Wars, Union League, Sons of the Confederacy. George Washington feared the growth of these organizations, as he saw only partisan strife emanating from their activities, even if they were primarily ceremonial gatherings. Yet the officers of his army came together to form the Order of Cincinnatus, embarrassing the president into accepting an honorary membership. In response, those who had fought in the Revolution as infantry and other ground troops formed their own organizations and established parading groups that often mustered at the same times, July 4, Election Day, New Year's Day, and Washington's Birthday. Though they were not always invited to join the civic parades, they had a hierarchy and a way of ceremonially wearing their badges of office, generally making an ironic commentary on the high-toned fraternal organizations that preceded them. Commonly overlapping with working-class neighborhood or parish organizations, they often paraded themselves as servants of civility, as firemen, policemen, and so on. And in their neighborhood celebrations a different and much more bumptious approach was observable in their holiday deportment. While these groups continued to cluster around taverns and, as they became more settled, their lodge halls, they continued to think of themselves as representing the "real people" in contrast to the clubs of the prominent.

The companionable club background underscored in Mardi Gras came to New Orleans with the ascent of the Cowbellion Society, conceived by Michael Krafft, a Pennsylvanian transplanted to Mobile, Alabama. He and his friends left the Old Southern Hotel after ringing in the New Year and happened on Partridge's Hardware Store. Whether they purloined them or paid cash on the barrelhead, they mustered their arms, hoes, rakes, cowbells, and gongs and proceeded to march the streets raising proper hell, making their way to the home of the mayor, where they were greeted in the spirit of the season and invited in for a collation. As they later reported of their "Escapade," they elected to repeat the experience each year. After a few years the self-appointed "Midnight Revelers" changed their title to the "Cowbellion de Rakin Society," drawing due attention to their primary noise-making instrument. In 1835, it would seem, they brought their midnight reveling to New Orleans and rolled forth a parade with a title and subject: "Heathen Gods and Goddesses."

That they or their followers were making claims of originality for their carousing show is evident. But cowbellions under many other names, more usually called Antiques and Horribles or Callithumpian Bands, were to be found at New Year's and wedding shivarees all over the United States and Canada. They were far from original in practice or costume, for this was the customary way the year was brought in throughout Great Britain and many other spots in Europe, under the name of mummers or guisers, first-footers or skimmington riders. Whether they were of the elite or the working class, when they got in their cups they made toasts and other speeches drawing on the very kind of elevated oratorical language that we see peeking forth in the Cowbellions.

Skimmingtons, rough music, shivaree, tin-panning, belling, riding the rail, raising a ruckus, locking out, locking in are all terms for crowds as they come together in riotous and sometimes destructive celebration; and they are all ways of discovering the standards of everyday life for handling disruptive actions. And the groups doing this have equally bumptious names: belsnicklers, mummers, guisers, and the aforementioned Calithumpian Bands, which can still be heard in local festivals in New England and the upper Midwest. Sometime these groups and their activities emerge from the pure joy of common and intense experiences together at times of seasonal or life passage. Events such as these are notable for being ephemeral and for using objects and materials that are used up by the end of the revelry. As rites of consumption they call into play the most slapdash constructions. They commonly draw attention to themselves through that most short-lived of all sensory data, the loud noise. Firecrackers and other noisemakers, bonfires, torches, and candles are only the most obvious self-consuming artifacts deployed at these moments. They also use everyday objects, like pots and pans, brooms and sheets, out of their usual contexts, or draw on bird's nests, leaves, or other "natural" coverings as the basis of their costumes.

This very ephemerality of the objects, like cowbells and tin horns, calls attention to the noisiness, the use of fire of one sort or another, and the topsy-turvy character of the activity. The message is clear that that this is a cockamamie world that calls out for everyone's participation. The objects lend themselves to political and social statements of resistance, especially within the commercial world so tied to valuing more permanent goods. Tearing things up and piecing them together, so characteristic of the clown's motley costume, is simply one of the ways attention is drawn to the spirit of spontaneous celebration that pervades these proceedings. By their very character, they are jerry-built.

These organizations or others like them were also common on the frontier when the farmers found themselves unable to obtain title to their land. Often branded as local rebellions and even wars, such organizations of resistance, sometimes using the same sort of motley outfits as disguises, commonly calling themselves by some pseudo-Indian name; like the group that rejected the tea tax in Boston and named themselves Mohawks, they had themselves a merry old time. Reports of their meetings do not differ substantially from those of the famous Tuesday Club of Annapolis so fully reported by the Scots physician Dr. Alexander Hamilton.

But in New Orleans the cowbell and other such beaten-metal instruments took a special place in the revelry on the other side of town. For here, musicians from among the slaves and freedmen around Congo Square used just such struck metal devices not as noisemakers but as musical instruments played in the African style. The distance between the noisemaking Cowbellions and the singing, dancing, and celebrating slaves in Congo Square is all the world of difference.

Even with the pernicious inequities between those of European and of African descent, a significant amount of cultural transfer occurred between the two. Common sense dictates that the practices and conceptual strategies that travel best are those which optimize adaptability to new local conditions. Also, the bearers of this technique of adaptation are those who historically have constantly had to make adaptations as a way to get by. Recent historical works have confirmed that this was so for those of Western European, trans-Mediterranean, and African heritage. As those born in the New World developed markets for single-crop agricultural products, enslaved workers developed their own food resources at the encouragement of the plantocrats. Not only did they raise African tubers, bananas, mangos, guavas, and cashews for their own diet, but also pigs, goats, sheep, and cows, which were then sold at the Sunday Market. Going to market established a regular release for some slaves, and while they were at liberty, they not only sold things but they entertained themselves with singing and dancing events.

In New Orleans there were many such clubs that entered into the Mardi Gras moment in a variety of ways, especially through second-line marches organized by one of these fraternal groups. In fact, these parades have come to be known by the name second-line. The first line, commonly called the main line, is usually launched by the Social Aide & Pleasure club of the neighborhood. Their parade begins there. Legislation seldom encourages these parades to wander into heavily trafficked areas outside their domain.

While the marchers therefore seem to have a preplanned route, going from one significant household or barroom to another, they do not necessarily confine themselves within the accepted bounds of the neighborhood. In fact, these parades are less about establishing a sense of turf than they are about knitting together the neighborhoods against the interests of outsider politicians, social workers, police, or drug dealers.

In this precarious time, after the linked disasters of flood and engineering and bureaucratic malfeasance, where vernacular neighborhoods are largely silent, where the wooden housing stock is in ruins or ominously marked by dark rings of flood lines, one wonders how that key aspect of Mardi Gras second-lines, one wonders how the neighborhoods that fostered the second-lines will be able to continue the brass band parades with sufficent numbers of marchers.

The venerable S & P Club tradition dates to the late nineteenth century. Its progenitor, the New Orleans Freedmen's Aid Association, was founded in 1865, with the goal of providing loans, assistance, counsel, and a means of education to newly freed slaves.

African Americans formed brass marching bands early in the country's history. They played at many civic and community occasions, even in Jackson Square at St. Louis Cathedral. But their dominant function was to play for the funeral services of the members of the S & P Club that initiated them. When the service was over, and the procession moved from church to cemetery, the band played sad hymns and dirges. On the way back, the music was joyful, with such high-spirited tunes as "Didn't He Ramble," and the second-liners dancing with abandon.

After the untimely demise of the New Orleans Freedmen's Aid Association, benevolent organizations arose within neighborhoods to function as mutual aid societies. Throughout the city there were fraternal groups and burial societies who often competed with one another to see which group could send off a member in the greatest style. The S & P Clubs of the early twentieth century provided (some still do) aid to fellow African Americans and ensured that club members get a proper burial. Several clubs founded before and shortly after the turn of the twentieth century are still around today. The Young Men Olympians was formed in 1884, the Zulus in 1909, and the Prince of Wales in 1928.

The clubs were operated like a social safety net—that's what "aid" means. A member paid dues each month, and could even borrow against it, with some clubs. If times were hard, they were the community's social services agency. But they had a very real limit. It was important to get on your feet again as quickly as possible.

Once the member's burial expenses are paid, the balance of the money is used to finance the funeral in style, sometimes, if desired, with a traditional New Orleans jazz funeral. Usually, the club hosts a jazz funeral, complete with a brass band and horse-drawn carriage bearing the casket. Members dress in matching suits with handmade decorative chest banners, called "sashes," and they carry elaborately decorated fans, umbrellas, and handkerchiefs. One member carries the club's official banner.

The S & P Clubs are known as the keepers of the second-line tradition. Each year club members assemble or make a new suit and host their annual second-line parade. With names like the "Jolly Bunch," "Money Wasters," "Lady Buck Jumpers," and "Golden Trumpets," the S & P Clubs played a vital role in the community during legalized segregation that created an entertaining counterpart to Mardi Gras.

From just before the turn of the century to the dawn of the Civil Rights era in the mid-1950s, African Americans were prohibited from enjoying the greatest free show on earth—Mardi Gras. They were prohibited from entering the French Quarter, or congregating or even parading on the main streets, until the late 1960s, and therefore most outsiders knew nothing about the innermost secrets of the second-line. So the Social Aide and Pleasure Clubs (a.k.a. second-line clubs) celebrated Fat Tuesday ("Carnival Day") in their own unique ways. It was the S & P Clubs, along with the "Black Indians" (now called Mardi Gras Indians) and "street bands," that provided black culture along the Claiborne Avenue neutral ground, from St. Bernard Avenue to Orleans Avenue, until the most famous and largest S & P Club arrived—the Zulu Club.

The Zulu parade of New Orleans' black middle class and elite community, founded in 1909 as a reaction to white stereotypes of blacks as "savages," is a Carnival activity rivaled in scope and visibility only by the Rex parade on Mardi Gras day. Zulu members dress in Mardi Grass skirts and "wooly wigs," put on blackface, and throw rubber spears and decorated coconuts to the delighted crowds. Working-class blacks, particularly those of French/Spanish ancestry downtown and African Americans uptown, also invoke images of "wildness" by masquerading proudly in stylized Plains Indians costumes.

The black "Mardi Gras Indians" are hierarchical groups of men with titles such as Big Chief, Spyboy, Wildman, and Lil' Chief who dress in elaborate bead and feather costumes weighing up to a hundred pounds. The best-known costume makers say that their costume patterns come to them in dreams, and they take pride in never repeating a color or theme from year to year. After months of time and money invested in sewing costumes and practice sessions at local bars, a dozen or more "tribes" appear early on Mardi Gras day to sing, dance, and parade through back street neighborhoods. Some of the black Indian "gangs" or "tribes," with names such as "Creole Wild West," "White Cloud Hunters," "Fi-Yi-Yi," and "Wild Tchoupi-toulas," herald their Native American ancestry and speak in aesthetic terms evaluated by the group for emotional intensity and knowledge of their "Indian spirits" and "customs." Their performance style, however, is essentially Afro-Caribbean, as expressed in competitive dance and song and the call-and-response chants that mark their foot parades. These chants are structured around group leader's call and responses often in English, such as

LEADER: —"Sewed all night and I sewed all day"
GROUP: —"My big chief got a golden crown"
LEADER: —"Just to look good on a Mardi Gras day"
GROUP: —"My big chief got a golden crown."

Some whole songs are based on a secret code language with possible elements of French, French Creole and Native languages, with responses like "Hey pocky way" and "Ja ca mo fee non nay." They also use standard tunes such as "Lil' Liza Jane" and "Shoo Fly" to improvise tales of their daring and exploits as they "go to town" on Mardi Gras day.

The late "Tootie" Montana, "chief of chiefs" of the Yellow Pochahontas tribe, paraded over fifty years. Legions waited outside his Eighth Ward house on Villiere Street each year to see Montana's annual costume creation. A lather by trade with considerable hand and engineering skills, Montana asserted that he "dreams" his costumes, in a manner consistent with African ritual and festival arts in the larger diaspora. Montana also took a role in combating policy abuse of the Indian tribes—notorious for not seeking parade permits for their improvised walks within and beyond the down river neighborhoods that have since been flooded and physically destroyed. In 2005, when Indians came out Uptown *sans* permit on the eve of St. Joseph's Day (March 19)—a sort of *mi-carême*, a Mid-Lenten break—it was claimed that someone had a concealed weapon and the police famously harassed the Indians with sirens wailing, shoving, curses on the tradition, and arrests. In a subsequent city council meeting demanded by the Indian confederation of tribes to discuss the police action, Montana, ill and frail, appeared to say the words, "this has got to stop." At which point he collapsed from a heart attack. It is said he died on "the battlefield," as Indian songs and chants heroically portray the historically violent ritual landscape of black Carnival. This attribution—followed by the largest wake and jazz funeral for an Indian leader—was made especially poignant since Montana had crusaded for tribes to eschew the knives and guns of violence, to "fight with the costume" and see "Who's the prettiest?" The tough social and artistic visionary Tootie Montana was until the end.

While the Mardi Gras Indians and the Zulu parade use Carnival to make statements about group pride through inverted stereotypes of Indian and African tribes, many blacks also work at the service of whites during the parading season. This practice reflects the postcolonial social structure of New Orleans, with its large black poor population, small middle class of some Creoles and whites, and powerful but socially and economically stagnant elite. Some black participants with the white krewes lead horses for major figures and captains in parades such as Rex and Momus. Others dress in pointed white hood and cloaks—almost medieval and klan-like in their bearing—carrying torches called flambeaux that light the way for night parades of old elite krewes such as Comus. (Before blacks gained admission to mask in nineteenth-century Trinidadian Carnival, the flambeaux carriers were all whites dressed in blackface.) The earnings of modern black krewe servants come from tips for doing this dangerous and dirty work along the parade route.

Carnival Along the Gulf Coast

Although smaller in scale and less widely known than the New Orleans Carnival, Mardi Gras in Mobile has been celebrated in various ways since the beginning of the nineteenth century. The Cowbellions were formed in the 1830s and later began ordering their costumes from Paris, but during the Civil War Mobile's public Mardi Gras was called off. In 1866, it was revived by a veteran named Joe Cain, who dressed that year as a mock Chickasaw Indian chief called "Slacabamorinico" and drove through the then-occupied city in a decorated wagon. On the Sunday before Carnival, Joe Cain is now commemorated with a jazz funeral procession. Various other Mobile krewes such as the Comic Cowboys and the Infant Mystics also date to the nineteenth century. The Order of Myths, the oldest krewe (1867), was modeled after the early Cowbellions. The symbol of the Order of Myths, the last krewe to parade on Mardi Gras, is Folly chasing Death around a broken neoclassical column and flailing him with a golden pig bladder. Though this imagery is officially interpreted as a symbol of mirth's triumph over gloom, some suggest that the broken column originally alluded to the broken dreams of the Confederacy.

Black Mardi Gras in Mobile provides some counterpoint to all the above. Costumes and sometimes papier-mâché figures worn or made by African Americans or Afro-Creoles often draw on male and female figures who are ragged but elegant. The female "Molly" figure looks part courtesan, part high society lady, with a wistful look of lost elegance in sometimes torn and out of style clothes. Her male counterpart may wear a wrinkled stovepipe hat, fancy but wornout shoes, tattered vest, and patched dress pants. The couple is sometimes seen at the Joe Cain parade and other white marches and also as part of a separate black Mardi Gras parade that runs the gamut from black Masons riding in antique cars to fully realized images of Molly and her gent in papier-mâché. Mobile also has a small contingent of black brass bands hired to accompany all parades. The favored bands also play at the black Carnival ball, where the primary event is a series of counterclockwise mass walk-abouts to the brass band music, with maskers juking their umbrellas in a way that both celebrates and mocks high society.

The large official float parades in the Mardi Gras celebrations of both Mobile and New Orleans primarily represent Mediterranean and Caribbean traditions. The Mardi Gras Indians, plus newly revived walking groups of "Baby Dolls" (women who dress as little girls and "fancy" prostitutes) and "Skeletons" (men in black with white bones on their clothing and large papier-mâché skulls), along with the Zulu parade, suggest African and Afro-Caribbean influences mingled with European sources.

* * *

The Cajun and black Creole *courirs de Mardi Gras* of rural southwest Louisiana are linked to the expression of country French traditions brought by Acadians of Nova Scotia who came to Louisiana in the latter part of the eighteenth century. In a manner not unlike Christmas mumming in Europe and the Virgin and Leeward Islands, a band of masked male revelers goes from house to house on the open prairie land of southwest Louisiana. The men, on horses or flatbed trucks, dress as clowns, thieves, women, and devils. Some wear the traditional pointed capuchon hats with bells and streamers. The group is led by a *capitaine* who may wear an elegant silk costume in the Cajun bands (or simple work clothes in some black Creole Mardi Gras bands). The Mardi Gras bands come as quasi-vigilantes in search of *charité* (charity) in the form of live chickens, rice, spices, cooling grease, sausages, and other ingredients for a gumbo supper.

The capitaine, standing apart from the group as a keeper of the law, tries to prevent the men from becoming too disorderly or drunk and make certain that they carry out their agreed-upon rounds for the day. At each farmstead visited, the capitaine or a flagman arrives ahead of the band to see if the household will receive the Mardi Gras. There is usually an affirmative response to the courtly request "Voulez-vous recevoir cette band des Mardi Gras?" ("Will you receive the Mardi Gras band?"), whereupon the clowns are waved on to charge the house on horseback. Men in costume pursue elusive chickens through the muddy rice fields of early spring, leaping fences and crossing pig sties. After a chicken is caught, it is killed and put with other spoils in a sack, which is sent back to the village, where the cooking begins at midday. As the Mardi Gras runners depart a house, they sing a word of thanks and invite the householders to the dance and communal supper to be held in town or at a rural club late in the night.

The Mardi Gras song is significant because it is sung in a minor mode, and is reminiscent of medieval French folk music, generally not found in Cajun music today. Sung in French and usually performed by musicians who ride in a sound truck, it also contains a description of the Mardi Gras band's activities. Translated into English, the song is as follows:

The Mardi Gras Song

The Mardi Gras riders come from everywhere
All around, around the hub.
They pass once a year
To ask for charity
Even if it's a potato.
A potato and some cracklins.
The Mardi Gras riders are on a long voyage
All around, around the hub.
They pass once a year

To ask for charity
Even if it's a skinny chicken
And three or four corn cobs.
Captain, captain, wave your flag.
Let's go to the other neighbor's place
To ask for charity.
You all come meet us.
You all come meet us.
Yes, at the gumbo tonight.

By the end of the afternoon the band heads back toward "the hub," or starting point, in rice- and soybean-growing and cattle-raising towns like Mamou, Church Point, L'Anse Maigre, and Swords. The horseback riders may enter at a gallop. Those who are still sober enough entertain waiting crowds with stunts and various acts of bravado. The gumbo from the day's catch is served to the riders and the general public followed by a large dance ending at midnight and the beginning of the Lenten season.

The parallel black Creole Mardi Gras bands are often located near the Cajun towns in tiny rural settlements established in the nineteenth century by *gens de couleur libres* (free people of color), manumitted slaves, and other people of color. The black Creole Mardi Gras celebrations are usually smaller, involving ten to twenty men, more intimate and more traditional than today's Cajun courirs. The cowboy style of Cajun Mardi Gras has not taken hold in the black Creole community. For example, the black bands take great care not to trample house gardens or urinate in public while pursuing the fowl. Elders are helped down from their flatbed trucks by younger men, and the bands present themselves more as polite beggars than as vigilantes. The older men especially take great stock in such details and are critical of young ones who do not behave or sing properly. The black Creole Mardi Gras song is similar to that of the Cajuns, but is often performed in a call-response manner (revealing possible Afro-Caribbean influences commingled with Catholic chanting styles).

The usual response line to the leader's song is "Ouais mon/bon cher camarade" ("Yes my/good dear friend").

The question of how the Cajun and black Creole courirs interrelate has been controversial on occasion. From the Creole point of view, the Cajun bands are unruly and lacking in *politesse* (politeness). The majoritarian style of the Cajuns is further regarded with suspicion and sometimes fear by Creoles out with their band of revelers as they encounter the Cajun groups. In part this is because Cajuns often hold positions of power over Creoles, tending to be sheriffs, landowners, bosses, store operators, and so on. The Cajun Mardi Gras may also evoke images of the nineteenth-century prairie vigilante and night-rider. Creoles, for their part, occasionally dress as whiteface clowns and "Klu-klucks," and so parody the history of violence and dominance on the prairie.

The center of some local community and scholarly interpretive controversy has been the blackface figure in many (but not all) Cajun Mardi Gras called the *negresse*—a grotesque black female impersonator, usually with padded breasts, perhaps a "pregnant look," and such features as a tight dress, a rolling pin as weapon, and hair curlers. The negresse, taken mostly from archaic "ugly man" travesties found throughout North America, is portrayed variously as apelike, aggressive, comic, unreasonable, sexually powerful, wily, and dumb. Anger or at least concern sometimes arises about the negresse figure. Some Cajun community leaders and local scholars have defended the figure as simply part of the tradition with no offense intended. However this defense has not been without controversy. At least one visiting parish priest has criticized the image to his congregation—only to find many of them in revolt, not inconsistent with Cajun anti-clericalism regardless of the issue.

Some Cajuns have pointed out that black Creole Mardi Gras groups are portraying the white stereotyped figure of the klansman; however, the Klan and related local variations did exist in rural French Louisiana, while the negresse is a wholly created stereotypical figure that addresses race and gender in a carnival setting. The controversy has been further enflamed on occasions when black outsiders less familiar with the rural French Louisiana rules of association have sought to attend Cajun Mardi Gras as riders or tourists on the band's hay wagons. A definitive, broadly acceptable treatment of the meaning of the negresse figure in Cajun Mardi Gras still seems unattainable to town folk and local scholars.

While old traditions and Carnival assemblies continue, new Mardi Gras groups, events, and locales continue to emerge to meet new social concerns and issues. And they continue to bend, twist, and toy with a variety of cultural heritages. In New Orleans, gay krewes and their French Quarter costume contests have become highly visible. The Krewe de Vieux in New Orleans and the Spanishtown Mardi Gras in Baton Rouge have sometimes become avant-garde satires, on Carnival itself and on Louisiana topics such as politics and pollution. In Uptown New Orleans, new groups of professionals with somewhat more progressive politics have formed the popular Krewe d'Etat, which mocks political figures in Louisiana and nationally. They make certain to call humorous attention to scandals and the bad behavior of public figures—elected or not. A women's krewe called Muses—of woman professionals and the next generation of middle and upper middle class—has surrounded itself with satirical symbols, including a red high heel as a float and an official medallion that at once mocks and embraces overly feminine style. Muses has made a move to a Doodah Parade-like sub-krewes that make fun of the black and white high school twirlers, flag corps, and cheerleaders.

During the 1980s, more clubs began to be formed for the sole purpose of "parading" and not the "social aid" aspect. A new wrinkle had been born in the culture. These clubs' purpose was not to render aid for burial, but to be the social affiliation fabric, the bonding agent, as it were, of their members. Clubs of the new era began to drop "aide" from their names and missions and were now strictly for the pleasure of the members. Therefore the tax category under which they operated also changed. Because they no longer rendered aid or benefit to themselves or others, they were now legally considered "Fraternal Orders, Brother and Sisterhoods," and bound a different set of codes.

Starting in the late 1990s, another page was turned in the Main Line culture, when Kings and Queens started to appear on the parade routes with the groups. Most are from other clubs or older members who are honored by the club, but some clubs have taken to honoring the city's most influential and famous. Another aspect of the modern Main Line is the arrival of floats, whereas a few years ago there were none to be found in most parades. Whereas in years past, a Main Line may have only covered a block or two, it could now stretch for several blocks. These African American clubs cannot by ordinance parade or celebrate two weeks prior to or on Mardi Gras Day, and most do not heavily advertise beforehand that they will be marching. Instead, they spread the word in their neighborhoods and disseminate route sheets. Some may sport custom handkerchiefs, while others opt for just plain white ones. It is up to each club how elaborate it wants to be.

Each club has its membership stop at set bars along the "parade route." This is not in order to drink alcohol, but rather to rest, drink some water, and take a restroom break if needed. More important, it brings patrons into the bars to allow the owner to take advantage of the opportunity to make a little profit from the Line. It is a holdover from the days long ago when the bars actually sponsored each and every float in the Tramp parade, which later was called the Zulu parade. Dixieland jazz or brass bands frequently join in the roving celebrations

Suburban Mardi Gras celebrations have become strong in recent decades. Children are included and excessive drunkenness or sexual suggestiveness is largely excluded. In the rural courir there is an increasing focus on using the event to teach young children—boys and girls—Cajun or Creole "heritage" rather than engaging in the trickery and drunken revelry of the all-male bands. Adjacent Anglo-American regions have also started Mardi Gras celebrations. Monroe, Louisiana., for example, held its first parade in 1985, and local fundamentalist preachers denounced the celebration as "devil worship."

* * *

Many wonder what shape Mardi Gras will take in 2006 throughout the Gulf Coast. The country Mardi Gras, except perhaps in the far southwest Louisiana parishes, should be unaffected. But one Mardi Gras Indian tribe has announced it will parade in Austin, Texas, where several members now live. Others are adamant that they will use the occasion to return to the city and express a revival of community life in New Orleans. Among the larger float parade-based krewes and in Mobile, an underlying assumption is that many will parade, though not in the size and scale of the past. Surely Katrina will be satirized as villainess, bimbo, or symbol of mythological flood. Political leaders at all levels will be taken to task. Mardi Gras will doubtless be a powerful if conflicted expression of the region's return to some kind of vitality and ability to express itself to itself and the world in the annual festive occasion of chaos and order in all its temporal and spatial variations.

As the new Mardi Gras evolves, it is appropriate to explore other elements of its cultural tradition, especially the terrain, location, and economic history of New Orleans.

The world seems to agree: New Orleans is not really an American city. It is a Creole city. Its language, foods, ways of dancing, and songs are all unashamedly filled with a French flair, a Latin tinge, and an African Caribbean sense of body and soul. We see this most fully in the various musics and dances that emerged from Greater Caribbean entrepôts—ports with highly mobile populations already mobilized through the vagaries of the transatlantic experience. Such ports of call served as a magnet not only for slavers and their human cargoes sold at the docks, but for the vagrants of the sea who labored as sailors, often against their own will. These were tropical gatherings of fugitives and outsiders living sufficiently beyond the control of metropolitan authorities to set up, in makeshift fashion, informal marketplaces. The plantation agricultural enterprises inland were capable of producing large amounts of surplus crops of sugar, tobacco, coffee, cocoa, rice, and other grains in which informal marketplaces would be opened in lands in between. It is not American in another dimension. It is an outpost of Caribbean culture that just happens to be on the mainland. New Orleans is an international port of call that has accumulated, along with the goods and services that are offered in such places, a wide range of peoples, most of whom not only have learned to live with each other as part of the Big Easy mystique, but have created a welcome for those visitors willing to take the city on its own terms.

Its language is born not of the place but of the plural population. That is, its culture is, on its face, the result of the coming together of many people in an environment that doesn't seem permanent. Not only are there many people and languages there, but the mix has created a great number of stylistic developments that, while clearly born there, are easily exported.

Yet, for all its international flair, it is a city anchored in its own terrain, as we have been reminded since hurricanes Katrina and Rita. It was a terrain of cultural interaction and creolization at every level, and this was seen dynamically in the rise, spread, and removal of markets in New Orleans. These markets simultaneously were built by creolization and complicated it in numerous ways. They were grounds for cultural inventiveness and locations for many marginalized peoples to take center stage.

Everything that makes New Orleans different seems to be centered on Congo Square, a market square that, like others throughout the Caribbean, is an exhibit of how to turn the most important orders of civil society into seeming disorder. For here the slaves seem to have become free, the low to have risen without putting the plantocrats on alert, and the place of everyday exchange to have been transformed, at least for the day, into a showplace of vivid consumption. And there, too, were the women who dressed up for this party, using the brightest and showiest techniques for them to show out.

Townsfolk would gather on Sunday afternoons to witness what went on inside the square. In 1819, Benjamin Latrobe—an architect fresh from restoring the Capitol after the War of 1812 and then in New Orleans to build the water works—wrote about these celebrations in his journal. He was amazed at the sight of five or six hundred unsupervised slaves who had assembled to dance. He described them as ornamented with a number of tails of the smaller wild beasts, with fringes, ribbons, little bells, and shells and balls jingling about the performers' legs and arms. The women, one onlooker reported, according to their means, clothed themselves with the newest fashions in silk, gauze, muslin, and percale dresses. The men garbed themselves in oriental and Indian dress and or covered themselves only with a sash of the same sort wrapped around the body.

Another witness pointed out that several clusters of onlookers, musicians, and dancers represented tribal groupings, with each nation taking its place in a different part of the square. In addition to drums, gourds, banjo-like instruments, and quillpipes made from reeds strung together like panpipes, marimbas and European instruments like the violin, tambourines, and triangles were used.

Just how unique this marketplace was is difficult to ascertain. One glimpse from Philadelphia of a time earlier than Latrobe's description of the goings-on in Congo Square indicates how widespread these gatherings may have been. John Watson, in his *Annals of Philadelphia*, records a conversation with a woman describing earlier days in that city, and in one of the major squares:

It was the custom for the slave blacks, at the time of fairs and other great holidays, to go there to the number of one thousand, of both sexes, and hold their dances, dancing after the manner of their several nations in Africa and

speaking and singing in the their native dialects, thus cheerily amusing themselves over the sleeping dust below. An aged lady, Mrs. H. S., has told me she
had often seen the Guinea negroes, in the days of her youth, going to the
graves of their friends early in the morning, and there leaving the victuals
and rum. (Watson *Annals*, 1: 406)

Yet it is Congo Square, and not Washington Square or any other place
north of Baton Rouge, that is taken to be the originating place, the
wellspring of Africa in the New World. Congo Square as the locus of
African culture in North America can be discerned in numerous ways.
It is discoverable, over and over, in those few descriptions we have of
Congo Square, a place long since covered over, developed, redevel-
oped, and finally, made into a civic park for tourists to visit.

The descriptions by Latrobe and others of festivals and festivities
are not that unusual in the travel literature of their times. Many others testify with surprise at finding themselves surrounded by such a
scene, in Charleston, Savannah, and Albany as well as throughout the
Antilles, in French, Spanish, and English colonies. These performances of culture arose at open spots in the urban landscape, at holiday times, or on the Sabbath. They provided a number of liberties to
the enslaved populations: an income, a chance to dress up, a time to
sing and dance, sometimes seemingly in reunion with others of the
same "nation." And in the evening, in this quarter at the edge of the
city, more formal dances would be held, often balls for which atten-
dees had to obtain a ticket, yet another sign of the organization and
integration of the alternative economy of the slaves.

Outside observers, when they first encountered these markets and
the events around them, registered astonishment time and again.
They were surprised at the noise and the music, at the number of
those attending, and at the high style of dressing (often described as
"the latest fashions," but using color combinations and textures that
challenged any Parisian style).

Conditions in the marketplace magnified the instability of creole
outposts. In the Old World, in both Europe and Africa, trade was carried out at periodic fairs and markets, often by bringing together

merchants from many places. These markets would open in a locale for a few days and were therefore not subject to the legal systems of the sedentary members of the host community. Whether in the Old World or New, all such markets shared the characteristic of tumult. They were locations of noise and unpredictable movement, and of pickpockets, con men, prostitutes, musicians, streetcorner orators and sermonizers, journeyman mechanics, and itinerant preachers of all sorts. The customary practices of this sort of market were geared toward quick-hit sales and chance engagements. Anthropologist Marshall Sahlins notes that here "negative reciprocity" is the norm— "the unsociable extreme" of exchange behavior in which attempts are made to trick, cajole, unbalance customers and vendors alike through creative deceptions, so that those involved can feel they have gotten something for nothing. Such markets contrast markedly with exchanges carried out within the family or the community, which are often surrounded with ritual gestures, with the goods exchanged confirming or transforming relationships.

The traders that followed the privateers and the first settlers knit themselves into European markets, even as they altered the ways production and consumption were carried out. Both fear and wonder were contained in the profusion of goods and the mixture of peoples engaged in these practices. A real social and physical fear of contagion centered on the actual sites of market exchange throughout the expanding emporium economy. The presence of traders in exotic garb further intensified this sense of strangeness at the point of exchange. If business were not so central to market going, it could be accused of being a play world. All the devices of play—fear, risk, contests and open conflicts, dizziness and other disorienting techniques, and, of course, the occasional strolling players or puppeteers—were encountered.

Under conditions of enslavement, both on the sea and in the new colonies, an even more comprehensive set of fears was introduced. The greater the number of languages used in carrying out this trade, the higher the possibility of secret cabals that might betray the order of the official worlds. Getting rich and consorting with the Devil often seemed the same thing, as planters and their agents were enriched by their ventures. White Creoles came to be associated not only with vast wealth, but also with spiritual slovenliness, overeating, laziness, insanity, brutality and double-dealing—all characteristics associated with whites' views of people of color as well. In fact, the plantation records and diaries written by overseers and doctors confirm that sexual indignities were widespread. The promised New World riches of which European investors and adventures dreamed were often overshadowed by the anxieties attending overseas settlement. Travelers' reports expressed these fears when discussing French and British tropical and semitropical enterprises. One source of this fear and fascination with depravity and decadence lay in the traumatic engagement with frontier conditions. Plantations may have been conceived as rational agricultural enterprise, but in practice the civilizing process itself underwent a test as a variety of humans came together, the issue of an unstable blend of upward-striving, dislocated metropolitan Europeans, indentured servants, native peoples, and enslaved Africans.

Few of these freebooters and adventurers developed any love of the land or allegiance to a patria in the New World. Home for many planters remained London or Paris, while for many in the enslaved populations a generalized Africa remained the place to which their spirits were consigned in death and burial ceremonies. Historian Ira Berlin calls the ambiguous figures who emerged within this system "Atlantic creoles," designating their point of origin as the west coast of Africa where commercial "intermediaries, employing their linguistic skills, and the familiarity with the Atlantic's diverse commercial practices, cultural conventions, and diplomatic etiquette to mediate between African merchants and European sea captains. . . . Others played fast and loose with their diverse heritage, employing whichever identity paid best." To push this perspective a bit farther, it would not be a great leap to conceive of Creole culture emerging in shipboard life, especially among the able bodied seamen who hailed from so many different places.

New World colonizing experiences were multiply cursed, it seemed to many: market people allegedly kept multiple accounting books, and, even worse, were said to lie and fast-talk in face-to-face encounters. The actual processes of market trading were more complicated. They strained the limits of language and other modes of expressive exchange. Within the strange lingua franca endemic to trade, new methods of interacting between different enslaved peoples developed, a mode of communication sometimes regarded as a secret by the masters and overseers. Different kinds of exchange also emerged as those carrying different modes of expression intermingled—people with a variety of ways of expressing themselves, both within and outside the market zone, especially in their self-generated entertainments. Thus the Creole world represented mixing upon mixing, from more or less secret sexual and social intercourse to public imitations of one another's stylized festive and other expressive practices.

Europeans often found themselves in situations in which their inherited customary practices—especially those surrounding family units—were not responsive to their altered circumstances. Most plantation settlements were established without European women and children. Just as the technology of cultivation suitable to the climate and crops developed and spread from one settlement to the next, so, too, domestic practices of housing and food cultivation, preparation, and consumption altered for both slaves and masters. The darkest side of this social experiment—the brutal treatment of slaves—must also be regarded as a cultural development of the New World. Techniques of surveillance and control were conceived under conditions in which punishments found throughout Europe were made much more severe as Africans came to be regarded as property. The result from the perspective of all involved was regarded as unique and was widely referred to in terms of its creole character.

The surveillance and control involved in maintaining a plantation led, on the surface, to the dissolution of most vestiges of Old World cultures. Europeans were especially conscious of this devolution of civil norms among their own, and they did everything in their power to avert such an outcome. The cultural dislocation was especially profound within the slave populations. In the face of this deracinating principle, however, slaves developed a new mnemonic system, in which both Africa and the plantation found a place.

The ongoing historical and geographical disjunctions of the Creole experience continue to animate the present. Agents of empire and commerce created outposts on both sides of the Atlantic, audaciously mixing a wide variety of transient peoples, asking that they forge a society that would wrest tangible riches from these lands. It is no exaggeration to say that African forms were as deeply coded in their most intense moments of song, dance, and parade as were those of the English when they saluted visiting dignitaries, celebrated the King's Birthday, or conducted religious observances. Each group witnessed the other's public performances, so imitation went both ways across cultural boundaries.

Travelers were dispatched to judge the success of these enterprises in the expansionist experiment. Their appraisals focused not only on economic matters, but also on the relative success of carrying the benefits of civilization to these outposts. Whether or not the commentators saw the enterprise as successful, all commented in one way or another on the customs and mores of the creole people they encountered. Some, like the polemicists Daniel Defoe and Ned Ward, used the occasion to play on fears of cultural difference. Others attempted to woo new settlers through the promise of material, political, and social gain.

In 1779, soon after the Spaniards assumed control of New Orleans, they constructed the city's first market building—the French Market. This put an end to the levee and street corner markets. While protecting consumers from high prices and poor quality food, the establishment of the French Market also provided the Spanish government with increased control over local commerce. From this, a network of municipal public markets was born that survived numerous administrations: Spanish, American, Confederate, and American again. Throughout the nineteenth and into the twentieth centuries, it thrived. By the First World War, there were thirty-two markets scattered throughout the city, with at least one in every neighborhood. Their names testified to the diversity, including Memory, Suburban, Le Breton, Lautenschlaeger, Prytania, and Tremé. These markets served as economic engines in their neighborhoods and also reflected the cultural dynamics of the neighborhoods and the metropolitan area.

At the end of the nineteenth century, immigration in sheer numbers and diversity through the port of New Orleans matched that of New York and San Francisco. For many immigrants, the public markets provided an entry point into the economy as small-scale entrepreneurs. Many of the city's corner groceries and food processors began as stalls at the public markets. Shoppers would have to be prepared to conduct business in many languages—French, French Creole, African languages, English, Spanish, German, Gaelic, Chocktaw, Greek, Maltese, and Italian. Stall rents were low and shoppers were plentiful. Cheese mongers, fish mongers, butchers, green grocers provided New Orleans shoppers with basic necessities—*calas tout chauds* (fried cakes), pralines, *estomac mulâtre* (gingerbread), sassafras filé powder (for gumbo), and po'boy sandwiches.

Cultural interaction and invention continued to mark the city and markets. Sicilian truck farmers from St. Bernard Parish carted in crops like Creole artichokes, tomatoes, garlic, and fava beans. Hunters would bring in everything from raccoons, bears, and possums to live Painted Buntings ("the poor man's Canary") and dead birds of prey. Painter John James Audubon noted in his journal his surprise to finding "a Barred Owl, cleaned and exposed, for sale at twenty-five cents." Coastal fishermen, hunters, and trappers,—many originally from the Canary Islands, China, the Philippines, Croatia—would market oysters, shrimp, crawfish, muskrats, nutria, and a wide selection of fish.

Throughout the city, scattered remnants of the public market system remain. Some have been transformed into commercial businesses; others remain vacant or have been torn down. The nation's oldest continuously running public market—the French Market—remains open for business. In the heart of the Vieux Carré, it continues to draw large crowds to its weekend flea market, restaurants, and vegetable sellers. The St. Roch Fish Market continues to serve a mean gumbo. But at the beginning of the twenty-first century, this is all that remains of the once thriving and inventive public market system.

As markets have been created and recreated, fluctuated and stagnant, Mardi Gras has remained an ever present part of the economic, social, and cultural reworkings of the city. It is a creolized festival centered in sites, on the ground, and in particular locales, and it is a creation of that shifting and enigmatic city space we call New Orleans.

*   *   *

If the markets of New Orleans seem defined by their impermanent permanency, their consistent inconsistencies, and their profane sacredness, so too has Mardi Gras appeared temporary and enduring, stable and unstable. In this way, it has long mirrored the city itself. New Orleans is a city built on the shifting mud of a delta beside waters that change directions, especially during floods, and it is famously below sea level and between a lake and a swamp. The fine regional writer George W. Cable described the founding of the city by the Brothers D'Iberville in his 1884 book *The Creoles of Louisiana*:

The year before Bienville [D'Iberville] secured this long-sought authorization to found a new post on the Mississippi he had selected its site. It was immediately on the bank of the stream. No later sagacity has ever succeeded in pointing out a more favorable site on which to put up the gates of the great; and here—though the land was only ten feet above sea level at the water's edge, and sank quickly back to a minimum height of a few inches; though it was almost wholly covered with a cypress swamp and was visibly subject to frequent, if not annual overflow; and though a hundred miles lay between it and the mouth of a river whose current, in times of flood, it was maintained, no vessel could overcome—he, Bienville, changed from the midshipman of twenty-two to the frontiersman, explorer and commander of forty-one, placed a detachment of twenty-five convicts and as many carpenters, who, with some voyageurs from the Illinois River, made a clearing and erected a few scattered huts along the bank of the river, as the beginning, that which he was determined later to make the capital of the civilization to whose planting in this gloomy wilderness he had dedicated his life.

Mardi Gras New Orleans style came into being with a kind of antic doom embedded in it. It signified life lived with one's back to the wall, where everything seemed extremely temporary and catastrophes of some sort would grow from the revelry.

After Mardi Gras is over, the event seems like a machine for making trash to many onlookers and those who do not know its heart. This contrast is experienced yearly: every aspect of life is subsumed in the moments of play, display, parading, and passing the bottle. The elements of Carnival may seem disparate and disconnected, yet the whole has an integrity and a spirit that draw in every way on the historic past. The two styles that define its heritage—the mumming in European traditions and the ring-dancing and singing of African and Caribbean traditions—emerge from different parts of the Old World, yet they merge seamlessly because they share the license to invert, to turn the social world topsy-turvy. Moreover, the costumes, shared excitement, frenzy, and disorientation of the moment are common features in any such festivity, shared in the Afro-Caribbean Junkanoo and the European Kermess. And both arise at the marketplace, that everyday area in which the rules of everyday, expressive exchange are challenged on a regular basis. Scholar-observer John Lohman makes fun of the disorientation when he points out that, with the wide-scale acceptance of the mobile telephone, it is not unusual to hear someone, like John himself, say "Hello. Where am I?"

Everything at Carnival is "of the moment," yet also of a long, sordid, beautiful past, arising out of flashpoints and calling for acts that seem to be destructive. All the experiential dimensions of play are brought to high pitch, inasmuch as they call for the consumption of a good deal of the material capital of the community. Yet the atmosphere attracts revelers operating in the spirit of celebration patterned on activities invented in time immemorial. Activities are as new as today's headlines and yet as old as the hills—or the levees. Everything seems to be new-made, but in a way that feels archaic. This is because Mardi Gras carries its own history from within its performance, and its own set of meanings.

Mardi Gras and its blood relatives emerge out of the places in the calendar that are marked as belonging to the otherwise beleaguered. If we are accused of making these high experiences into African American moments, it is because that has been the explanation of them by the participants since before Emancipation. And the African style of invention and improvisation continues to provide the girding and the spirit of these festivities, especially in the music and dance forms that become the signature styles of these high times. The features of Mardi Gras in New Orleans intersect with all the stylistic inventions of Carnival and of Junkanoo and the West Indian Christmas. By underscoring the continuities between Africa and the Caribbean, we are not suggesting that all the experiences of Carnival ultimately can be traced back to Africa, To the contrary, we see the events and process as creole inventions, styles emerging also from the contact between the many cultures that came together in these outposts: Spanish, French, British, German, Italian, Greek, Lebanese.

In the devastation of hurricanes Katrina and Rita, the celebration of impermanence may now achieve further ironic developments, since the mud, water, and bodies of the dead descended on the lowest parts of New Orleans and became national and international news. Similar natural and historical cataclysms have been visited on Port au Prince and Santo Domingo, Martinique and Guadalupe, and Port-of-

Spain, yet these places have reemerged after wars and political repressions of various sorts, as well as from hurricane winds, floods, fires, volcanic eruptions, and the diseases that seem to follow disasters. And in the aftermaths they have reinvented their carnivals and festivals.

Could Mardi Gras die? What would happen if Mardi Gras did not come back to New Orleans? Having created a vortex at the end of the Mississippi, and yet maintaining its deep connection to its related occasions in the rest of the Greater Caribbean, has the Carnival gone down in its own deep-sixing? Obviously not. Mardi Gras is much too lively and expansive an event not to be remade along with the city. Mardi Gras has already traveled so far and engaged such widespread interest and involvement that it could not fall to the power of hurricanes or inept politicos. And now, since Carnival has capitalized on its touristic potential, it has a life outside New Orleans. Perhaps it belongs, second hand, to those who get the videos and the images put forth by national and state radio and television.

The locally produced inventions of Mardi Gras prove to be of the sort that can be imitated in other festive environments. This is the case of most Carnival celebrations throughout the rest of the Black Atlantic—Jamaican, Bermudian, or Carolinian Junkanoo. Effects, images, and ideas are exported into Mardi Gras or Carnival elsewhere. A quickly and totally sharable vocabulary of motives and meanings cropped up wherever the plantation world demanded the development of a point of arrival and departure for the goods produced. These also happen to be those places in which periodic markets emerge.

The intensity of creolization is directly proportional to the distance between a colony and the metropolitan seat of power, and this relationship has led to curious interactions of markets and men, technologies and technocrats. The encouragement to creolize may in fact be felt by those feeling most alienated from the centers of political control. At such points, verbal combativeness or competitive games may be used as equalizing forces under even the most repressive situations, especially in the plantation world, where the calendared holidays were consistently seized upon by the lowliest and used as a time of inversion. The scene was thus set for extremes of celebration by the encouragement of all the bodily experiences of play: risk, wagering, coercing, drunkenness, strange dressing, fashioning up or dressing down, wearing masks or some other vestment that underscores that different roles are subject to being taken on by anyone. The entire Carnival was about presenting or enacting inversion, making night day and day night, through devices of illumination and explosion.

Why were these cultural and social inversions permitted? From time to time, metropolitan authorities attempted to prohibit or police the festivals, only to find the flashpoint moving to another part of the landscape. Perhaps the body politic needs this annual traumatic intervention as confirmation of the otherwise hegemonic system of deference, demeanor, and condescension. Civilization, at least for the British, was embodied in learning good manners. These holidays were, and are, an exercise in bad manners, or at least in subverting good manners. They are a time to act rude, to drink with reckless abandon, to celebrate disorder, and to get as close to a riot as could be contained by the rules of the festivity. Thus the need to have a "lord of misrule." Need we point out that there was a constant fear of slave uprisings or bread riots or ritual hangings and burnings in those gatherings? The symbolism of order and reorder are omnipresent at, especially as market towns often call for the creation of secret or hidden voluntary associations, groups that are only seen on days of celebration.

On the other hand, perhaps those in control get bored and desire the festival, not as a safety valve, but as a time to romp and play themselves, to cast off the shackles of their own self-imposed oppression. Perhaps the elites witness the creative efforts of even the lowliest and merely want to engage in the active cultural back and forth that occurs under playful conditions. Reshuffling the social deck of cards may present both ruler and ruled a time for fun. All kinds of hell can be conjured at the edge of civilization, but in a market town the tumult almost always arises in the market quarter and involves an enlargement of everyday market behaviors. And these behaviors are usually regarded as close to the edge of disorder by the authorities. The market, the area in which everyone is equalized at the moment of exchange, is where visibility is as important as mobility, even to those involved in making a steal.

Conclusion: Mardi Gras Will Never Die

The conditions after Katrina and Rita demand that vernacular creativity and the basic rules of creolization be brought to bear on the situation. Improvisation, community bricolage, breaking, and calling out provide the pattern for a future, whatever the details. The world is still there to be turned on its head. Perhaps the clean-up itself will take its pattern from the way in which Mardi Gras traditionally ends.

After the last float passes, Carnival comes to an abrupt end for those who have endured the entire time. Incredibly strong spotlights are directed at the area where there are the greatest number of stragglers—the effect isn't unlike the house lights coming up in a theatrical performance, except that the lights are accompanied by loud noises emanating from the police chief, mayor, or head of the clean-up crew. The message that the festivities now are ended creates a point of passage: everyday rules are once again in force, and, for those who have made this a holy experience, this is Ash Wednesday and the churches open at dawn. As John Lohman put it, this provides an unmistakable transition between "parade" exuberance and the "not parade" beginning of exhaustion, a last sigh effect.

Following each major parade, a fire engine and police cars burst onto the scene with sirens blaring, followed by men dressed in orange. Trustees of the Parish Prison, these men dismount unshackled from white Orleans Parish prison buses with wire mesh over the windows. As guards watch, the men fan out with rakes and they collect the refuse at a quick march: the go-cups, the bottles, the broken beads, the paper trash, and the rest of the year's gaudier throws gone awry in the gutter. All this material is piled into a growing trash line in the street, where a gigantic vacuum machine sucks it up at 5 miles per hour. Behind the prisoners and the sucking device are water trucks hosing away the effluvial leftovers, transforming the scummy sheen to a now-just-after-rainfall look.

The city, infamous for the inefficiencies of its public services, is ironically well known for making a street look like no parade had been there fifteen minutes after its conclusion. They do this with a strangely military intrusion, now with the elected and appointed civic officials on top, law enforcers in the middle, and those at liberty to sweep the streets at the bottom, wearing the bright orange vests commonly worn by highway cleaning crews.

As folklorist and master reveler Lohman noticed, even amid the cleanup there is a counter-Carnival operating as the city comes to closure on the festive season. Mardi Gras has ended, but another festivity of order-in-disorder, of social norms turned topsy-turvy, evolves. This counter-Carnival is run by the officers of order, drawing on the work force of their prisoners. For these men in orange, it is their own festivity of street roving and work similar to that created by the singing garbage men who line the French Quarter and other districts every day with their call and response codes and chants of safety in work-timing and social criticism. For the denizens of the dawn, this is a "lights camera and action" time when they receive cheers and a whiff of freedom for racing down the street behind a Carnival parade, and, they at the bottom of the social order, get cheers for removing the remains of the monarch's treasury.

Until a few years ago, the city of New Orleans rated carnival success in terms of the amount of garbage collected. It was a perverse measurement system cooked up by the public works department to show how efficient they were with their prisoners and big machines. C. Ray Nagin, the current mayor, a reformer, undid this. He maintained that we should not be encouraging people to throw or leave trash in the street at Carnival time, and that trash collected is neither the measure of an orderly public event, nor its all-important impact on the economy. Why, then, the widespread feeling that Mr. Mayor will not win this battle in the long run, a fact made somewhat moot by the other problems he now has to face?

Still, for the prisoners out free for a night (most parades before Carnival day are at night) it's a clean sweep for work as pleasure. They haven't been seen during Mardi Gras, because the officials in charge of such matters have reasoned that, with one parade after another during the festivity, why would clean it up in time for to do it again?

The reassertion of absolute control of the city begins at midnight, when the mayor, police chief, and parish sheriff appear with a horse-mounted patrol at the top of Bourbon Street (at Canal Street). There, they declare "Mardi Gras is over! Please go home!" Then they ride the length of the French Quarter, repeating the announcement and followed by the prisoners, city vacuum, and water trucks. Of course not everyone agrees with officialdom: the next neighborhood down-river, Faubourg Marigny, has a sort of neo-Bohemian, indie-rocker Mardi Gras, complete with a mock crucifixion, fire eaters, and post-"Iron John" drum circles, promoting a final bedlam until the police, sometimes with clubs up, close it down at 4 A.M.

The role of performing the official end of Mardi Gras is a choice job for those entrusted with it. It also seems to make a mocking comment on the relationship between cleanliness, godliness, and social status. After Katrina, the chances of making a deeply playful ironic comment on cleanliness and contagion will surely be noticed by those who live to mock the ultimate vanity of parading and paraders.

On Mardi Gras day, the clean-up crews are not so "Johnny-on-the-Spot" relentless. As parades roll continuously and there are no more concerned locals or arriving tourists to impress, the detritus piles up. On Ash Wednesday, the city's main streets exhibit a wasteland of beads, cups, banners, confetti, and food. The long slow, clean-up day begins when the penitents flock to church seeking ashes (and per-haps forgiveness for all they did during Mardi Gras), while the prison-ers return to their demi-world. Lent cherishes cleanliness and godliness until the next festive outburst on the days of St. Patrick and St. Joseph, a couple of weeks later.

The way life is registered after Carnival and cleanup is no longer governed by the play rules in place during Mardi Gras. All the apparatus of festive appreciation, especially the symbolic and ironic way of viewing things, disappears. "The sirens are really loud and the lights are really unpleasant," Lohman reported. The environment is never totally changed, however. The marks of the Mardi Gras world are carried away by the performers, and they will retain these body memories that will serve them well next year. But also, as Lohman remarked to a fellow reveler, after the streetcleaning in the French Quarter and elsewhere in the Garden City, Mardi Gras itself seems to evaporate. The doubloons, the beads, and all the other trash swept away left something of a void for him. But a fellow-in-arms pointed out that the beads and other glitz were still hanging from the trees—a visual trail of objects having been played hard and played out.

Meanwhile, today in the flooded parts of town, the residents who are left look on knowingly, implicitly saying, "Well, we were never much of a part of that show. We had our own." On the West Bank where they held forth, the streetcleaning was never to be observed. There the parade loops back on itself at the end, sometimes creating a never-ending circle: last year it was so crowded and entangled that it created traffic gridlock. Here there are people, not trash trucks, in the streets all day and all night. For months residents will get a little nostalgic as they drive over the mounds of crawfish shells left behind in the streets. In the communities on the West Bank, Mardi Gras is not only celebrated on Fat Tuesday but year round, in its own way. "For New Orleans' black community, the boundaries between 'Carnival Time' and 'Everyday Life' are far more diffuse."

* * *

What will become of New Orleans and Mardi Gras? We cannot say for certain, but if the beads are any indication, there's a lot of staying power there. They will continue to be worn and given, received and cherished, cast away and reprocessed. One particularly sensitive businessman noticed, when he was allowed to return, that the mess was actually a "sign of progress." Doubtless he was already speculating on the opportunities created by what he saw as empty land.

On the other hand, Mayor Nagin, taking the chance to get out of town for a minute, was asked by NBC's *Meet the Press* whether New Orleans could stage Mardi Gras in February 2006. "I haven't even thought that far out yet," he said. But then he added, "It's not out of the realm of possibilities. . . . It would be a huge boost if we could make it happen."

Today, the staunch Mardi Gras Indians point to what is left, what will be renewed even if it is jerry-built, and to the pleasures and passions left behind by last year's revelers. Already another kind of parade is being lined out, one that will take bus passengers from one once-notable spot to another, telling tales of what used to be there, much like the ghost and vampire tours of the French Quarter. But, surely, the ideal of funky and resistant exoticism wasn't all washed away, nor was the combative spirit carried by the chant "Laissez les bon temps roulez." Some of the pleasure spots are gone, but, like Mardi Gras itself, they were constructed of found materials, and so they will be again when those who were the proprietors of such places hopefully return in full strength.

Meanwhile, some rural Cajun and Creole parish revelers, holding their stolen chickens aloft, boast that they are ready to take up the slack, if the crowds are willing to play their way. It is hard to imagine that they have enough horses, or even open trucks, to accommodate that many visitors, but they say they will damn well try, in French Creole or Cajun, even if the visitor doesn't understand either the words or their spirit and history right away. The Mardi Gras Indians now living in Austin, Texas, may move their parade to that other music city this year, but it will only add to the revels already going on Sixth Street every night.

What will happen in the streets of the Crescent City? Unlike the Phoenix, New Orleans will rise from mud, not ashes, after a trial by water and un-benign political neglect, not by fire. The future of an authentic Land of Dreams is in the hopes and will of the people who have always made it the Creole heart of America's soul.